Your Solar Return

A Living Diary of Life
Through the Annual
Solar Revolutions

Cynthia Bohannon

ISBN-10: 0-86690-618-5
ISBN-13: 978-0-86690-618-0

First Printing: 1997
Current Printing: 2011

Published by:
American Federation of Astrologers, Inc.
6535 S. Rural Road
Tempe, AZ 85285-2040

www.astrologers.com

Printed in the United States of America

Dedication

This book is dedicated to the
Guides of the Solar Return
and the twin spirits Ovensy and Lester
who in concert with one another have brought forth
to the world with patience and devotion
this masterful work.
It is a gift of love for humankind
as they enter the threshold of the New Age.

"Astrology is assured recognition
from psychology, without further
restriction, because astrology represents
the summation of all
pschological knowledge of antiquity."

Carl Gustav Jung

CONTENTS

Planets in the Houses

YOUR SOLAR RETURN

This book is to be used from one year to the next, and if consulted regularly and used properly, the natural progression of life will be evident each solar year. This will enable the astrologer to determine for themselves and others whether they are making progress and how to avoid mishaps in their lives. With continued use, it becomes a learning tool and a mirror of the individual life.

It must be emphasized that the solar return information contained in this book brings an awareness and guidance that cannot be obtained with any other system. It is a natural progression of life, showing a trend as to where one has been and that which can be expected the following year. It prepares people to see their future, bringing an understanding of the events ahead. It provides an overview of problems or benefits that are expected to occur.

That which is to be experienced during the year is predicated on the outcome of the previous solar return. One who has experienced financial difficulties one year, for example, will find the problem eased the following year, provided the person has learned from the experience.

Individuals should choose to live in a beneficial and productive manner; thus, they can expect to overcome the pitfalls and to apply their benefits properly.—*Ted George, Associate Author, Editor*

*"Astrology is a science in itself and
contains an illuminating body
of knowledge. It taught me many
things, and I am greatly indebted to it.
Astrology is like a life-giving elixir for mankind."*

Albert Einstein

Chapter I

Erecting the
Solar Return Chart

For the solar return chart to be precise, the chart must be based upon the return of the Sun to its natal degree where the individual presently resides, using the time that existed at the new location. This is necessary for the reason that using the birth time and the co-ordinates for the place of birth would not work out precisely every year, unless the person continues to live within the same coordinates. There could be a large margin of error if the chart were made for the natal time and place, especially when using the transit of the Sun as it conjuncts the degrees of the houses and planets of the solar return chart.

One must also be aware that if a move is made midway through the solar return year, a new chart must be erected for the new place of residence.

The Ascendant Sign

The Ascendant will disclose where the most active part of the solar return will take place. It will also reveal the house that comes to the Ascendant of the solar return chart from the natal chart. The house of the natal chart bearing the same sign as the solar return

Ascendant will have a decided and important effect on the life of the individual.

It is important that the natal chart be interspersed around the solar return chart since the solar return represents the transits of the planets. This will aid in the interpretation of the solar return as that which the natal chart promises, the solar return brings.

Intercepted Signs

There are three areas that must be examined when intercepted signs occur in the solar return chart. They are: health concerns, the house of the interception, and a delay in the energies of the planets involved in the interception. The three areas are further explained as follows:

Intercepted signs in the chart will signify health problems in the areas of the body ruled by the signs intercepted. The health problems will surface no matter what house is involved.

The houses of the interception will also indicate health problems so that there would be two different health issues in connection with the interceptions. An interception in the third and ninth houses, for instance, can reveal a problem with those areas ruled by Gemini and Mercury, such as the nervous system, muscles, lungs, arms and shoulders. In addition, problems related to the blood, veins, arteries, hips and thighs are ruled by Sagittarius and Jupiter. However, there is also a secondary effect in that it can involve brothers, sisters, relatives, neighbors, and a minister or teacher who may be important in the life of the subject.

Planets positioned in intercepted signs do not work for the most part, nor do they bring forth their energies until after the Sun has passed the point of the interception, and this includes the faster planets Mercury and Venus, sometimes Mars. They function similarly to planets in retrograde motion.

Aspecting the Chart

It is the planet Uranus that is the most important and the aspects of the planets to Uranus. A planet in hard aspect to Uranus would be detrimental in the solar return chart, especially as we move closer into the Aquarian Age, but so would the easy aspects be fortunate for the subject. The personal planets would affect the individual on a day to day basis, but the general overview would be the placement of the planet Uranus.

Insofar as aspects are concerned, there will be heavy conjunctions of planets in one sign, thus concentrated in one area of the solar return chart. The conjunctions have an effect by aspect on all individuals, whether difficult or beneficial. Many groups will be experiencing the same events based upon the karmic effects of their society. As the New Age arrives, it brings about changes to the masses; therefore, there is a lineup of planets to affect groups of people and not just individuals. Each individual is a part of the whole, so heavy conjunctions will be frequently seen as the Aquarian Age displays its influence. The aspects are the same. Each planet of the conjunction should be aspected individually.

The solar return chart interpretations in this book are based on the Placidus system of house division. Many astrologers are using different systems of house division that would not lend themselves to these interpretations.

It is important to remember that interpretation of any astrological chart is based upon the individual who interprets the chart. Astrology remains the same with the interpreters basing the reading on their own system. The person who wants to see something in a particular chart will see it in some way in spite of the system used. But truly, astrology is astrology even though the interpretations are different.

The individuals who have been correctly trained in the use of the Placidus system of house division find they receive far greater results overall than with any other house system. It has survived all other systems over the centuries and it is a proven method for chart interpretation, especially for solar return charts where the houses and the degrees are of utmost importance.

The Solar Return Calendar

The solar return chart is an exciting calendar indicating that which can be expected to occur as the Sun conjuncts every house cusp, planet, and other positions throughout the year, beginning with the natal degree and sign. Consult an ephemeris for the dates that the Sun conjuncts all the points in the chart, and record the dates on the chart and on a calendar that is utilized frequently. As each date appears on the calendar, an occurrence will take place in accordance with the placement in question.

Events with respect to each position may occur the day before, on the day, or the day after the Sun conjuncts each point in the chart. It is interesting to note that persons will appear to the subject who has that position in the natal chart.

Transfer the chart to the solar return graph so that a record is kept of every chart. The graph will become a diary of the life as each revolution occurs over the lifetime.

Observing the solar return as the action unfolds at each placement is the best way to develop the technique of chart interpretation.

Important: A solar return chart should be erected for the year following the current year. Within three months prior to the end of the current year, the new year begins to take effect, so that there is an intermingling of the two charts as the year draws to a close. The influence of the new year does not override the current year, but is simply announcing its arrival before it begins to fully affect the life.

Health

The sign on the cusp of the sixth house, together with the dwad and its planetary ruler, will indicate any disorder that will afflict an individual during the year. Dwads are determined by each two and a half degrees of a sign, with the sign ruling the cusp representing the first two and a half degrees. For example, seven degrees Cancer on the sixth house cusp would indicate a problem with the stomach, but where the affliction is coming from can be shown by the Virgo dwad. It indicates the problem is caused by those matters ruled by the sign Virgo and Mercury, such as diet and the nervous system.

CHAPTER 2

Planets in the Houses

Sun—The Great Luminary

It is important to note the placement of the Sun in the chart as it illuminates the chart for the entire year.

The transit of the Sun in one of the first six houses is there to benefit the individual for the reason there has been difficulty with that house placement in a prior solar year. These houses are personally related and will be very positive for the individual.

With the last six houses it becomes important to note the lifestyle of the native, and the career and work, in order to properly evaluate the effect of the Sun in that particular house. It should be noted that as the new age arrives on the scene, the solar return will become very much more prominent.

Sun in the First House

This will be a pleasant year for the individual who is being rewarded for progressing through a difficult prior year. If the person has not experienced this placement in previous years, it is an indication that lessons have not been learned.

This brings about a cheerful and bright personality, and the individual has more energy than in previous years, as well as a radiant glow and a bright disposition with a positive outlook. Good fortune will be bestowed throughout the year.

This is a good time to take care of matters that have been plaguing the person, and to move forward with any projects left unfinished; success is now assured. If a serious health problem exists, the individual will now receive the benefit for the suffering experienced by finding the right path to health.

The mental outlook is greatly improved and if the individual suffered from depression in the past, he or she will find it hard to believe feeling so well now. The individual will be fortunate in all situations, with renewed vitality and recognition for what has been accomplished. Some will seek recognition and others will receive it, but above all it will be an exceptionally bright year.

Sun in the Second House

There will be financial gains and accumulation of possessions. The native is fortunate in dealing with banks and savings accumulate at a more rapid rate. Generally, this placement follows a year of previous financial problems due to health or other unfortunate occurrences. Because the individual dealt with the problems in a positive manner, the light in all matters of this house is being bestowed.

This is a time to accumulate wealth as there is an energy to accumulate more in savings, and possessions. It is necessary for the individual to save income as much as possible as it will be some time before there is freedom from financial problems created by prior solar years. This is a karmic benefit for the financial difficulties previously experienced.

If one does not experience this placement for a period of years, it indicates the individual has not satisfactorily worked through previous problems. This does induce the native to purchase possessions of some kind for others, or to benefit others through financial knowledge.

Sun in the Third House

This brings vitality, energy, and fortunate experiences with relatives, more in the nature of personal growth and development in dealing with relatives. The individual has an increased ability to communicate, and this is a fortunate time for the native to pass on knowledge on various subjects to others.

It is the year to write, teach, communicate, or indulge in short travels to accomplish goals. Those who did not have the ability to talk or communicate well now find they have the ability to express themselves; this also can take the form of writing. It is a fortunate time for the person to improve his/her knowledge and education and to pass on that knowledge on to others.

Sun in the Fourth House

This is a very fortunate position in that the individual finds it easy to deal with the dominant influence in his/her life. This would generally be the dominant parent or another person close to the native. There will be personal growth accomplished through learning to forgive and to love the dominant person. The individual will learn to love the home and appreciate that which has been received over the years.

This is the time to reflect on self and to learn about self from the past. The native will spend more time about the home as there will be more activity in dealing with all matters of this house placement. The individual can expect a dynamic year—much energy and vitality with respect to the home base, parties, people, and children, and a very good year overall.

It is an exceptionally good year to have a child. It would be a positive and enriching time. The native can expect dynamic things to occur to bring balance in the life. This would necessarily be determined by previous solar returns and whether the individual is progressing and developing in a positive and constructive manner. The individual should take advantage of this placement as it takes many years to return in the solar chart.

Sun in the Fifth House

There will be a great romance during the course of the solar year, together with a love of oneself. After years of not caring for self, the individual will learn to love self and others. It will be in the form of a lover or a child.

This is the year to enjoy life—to travel and pursue those things the native was unable to do in previous years because of ill health, injury, or financial restraints. If the native has worked hard to improve self and image, falling in love with someone at this time would turn out to be a great love affair that would last for many years.

Fortunate speculative adventures can be expected. Persons will find their investments have multiplied with winnings in games of chance. It is a fortunate time to pay attention to investment advice. It is also a fortunate time to purchase gold or to give gold as a gift to a lover. This is an extremely fortunate position.

Sun in the Sixth House

The individual finds a vitality that has been unknown for many years. This brings back energy previously known but thought lost. It is a good year for work, to be around other employees, and to be responsible for a pet or other animals. This is a fortunate time with respect to the working environment.

The native should try to do as much as possible in relation to work because working with this placement in a positive manner can be a truly renewing experience; that is, through self-development, self-awareness, and self-understanding. The individual will be greatly rewarded.

The native suddenly discovers benefits through alternative sources for good health, such as diet and herbs. The discovery is made that taking legal or illegal drugs has held the native back. It is possible that ill health and other problems could return if the individual does not continue living life in a positive manner.

There will be enjoyment in working and in keeping an exercise program. Since the person has more vitality with this position, the more physical exercise the better as long as it is in conjunction with a proper diet. Self-improvement and a life of continued positive influences will insure that the effect of this placement will last for far more than one year.

The next six houses in the solar return apply only for the year. The reason is that the effects pertain to others and to those matters outside of self. This is a growing and developing time for the individual.

Sun in the Seventh House

More time will be spent with a partner or the public, depending on the life of the individual. The type of work and lifestyle of the individual are important with this house placement. If the individual does not have a chosen career, law school may be uppermost in the mind. There will be more energy expended in socializing than was experienced in prior years. It brings an opportunity for a partnership but the benefits apply only to the other person and not to the native. This is also an opportune time to bring legal activity to a conclusion.

The individual enjoys partnerships more even though he or she is already married or in a business situation. Everything pertaining to matters of this house will have a positive influence for the person, but only for the solar year.

Sun in the Eighth House

Pleasure comes to the individual with respect to other people's money, the occult, and sex. There is a renewed vitality for sex for those who had no desire for it or no opportunity to enjoy it. It brings a renewed interest in one's sexual compatibility with a partner and in new ways of enjoying sex.

Vitality and energy are brought to the person in order to study the occult and the death experience. There will be an interest in inheritance or it will bring an inheritance of some kind to the partner, but not necessarily to the native. There could also be an interest in helping others involved with an inheritance. In any event, an inheritance would not happen many times during the lifetime of a person.

Sun in the Ninth House

This will be a time for studies of philosophy, higher education, and foreign travel. This is a fortunate time for the individual to take a trip for traveling would be thoroughly enjoyed. The native will have the vitality to travel and they will not experience problems connected with any form of travel.

As spiritual matters are important with this house, the individual should develop spiritual awareness. This is also an appropriate time to resolve any legal problems involving either the native or the partner.

This is the house of publishing, so it is a fortunate time to submit articles or manuscripts for publication. The person can successfully seek employment with a publisher or with a religious or educational institution.

Sun in the Tenth House

The individual can expect to receive a promotion, a raise in salary or recognition for his/her efforts. It is a time for advancement if the individual has developed self through experiences with the other house positions through previous years.

It is a time of great advancement and a fast rise to the top of the career. Many beneficial occurrences can be expected with respect to career and government if the individual is employed by any branch of government. Those that have worked on their spirituality, strength, and vitality will receive many benefits.

Sun in the Eleventh House

Energy will be expended with respect to friends and organizations. The individual will develop methods to increase income, or be involved with some type of scientific endeavor. This could be one who disliked science but who now has a better outlook on this subject. One who felt astrology was worthless now may find it a subject worth investigating.

This can be a fun year because of increased socializing and a greater interest in those areas the individual finds unusual. The native will be attracted to unusual friends, partnerships, or other interests where previously there was an interest. This is a very positive position despite the fact that it is only for a year. Those keeping a record of their solar returns will find that this is a position that comes around quite frequently in the solar return chart.

Sun in the Twelfth House
Contrary to what may be expected, this does bring favors. But it also brings out hidden enemies, and a lot of information the individual was not aware of, both self-knowledge and what pertains to others. Those who have been taking drugs find they now have the ability to discontinue using them.

It is a good placement for the individual to work out difficulties or to overcome any troubles. However, the benefits of this position are in effect for only a year so if the individual continues to indulge in illegal drugs or activities, luck will run out and the native will encounter unexpected trouble. He or she might be able to avoid trouble and play with danger for a year, but the favors of this placement end with the solar year.

This is a very good time to develop spiritual awareness or to be involved with psychics. Those with psychic ability will find this is a very good time to help others. It is also an appropriate year to help the less fortunate in some way.

If it is necessary for the individual to be hospitalized, he or she can expect to leave the hospital much sooner. This placement can prevent a hospital stay because of the native's extra vitality; the illness could clear up, thus eliminating the need for hospitalization. The person might enjoy visiting hospitalized people in order to brighten their days.

The lifestyle of the individual has much to do with the outcome of this position, as it does with the other five house placements.

Venus—The Charming Socializer

Venus is a beneficial planet that helps alleviate unfortunate aspects in the chart. It is considered harmonious where it is located, but it also brings indulgences with respect to a love of something or someone. It does bring joy and happiness where it is needed in the solar return chart.

Venus in the First House

The individual begins to enjoy life with this placement, more so than in previous years. The native is charming and social, with the vitality necessary to continue socializing throughout the year if there is a conjunction with the Sun. The individual learns social graces and how to be diplomatic.

This is a good position for the person to be a mediator for a group or organization. The individual will bring harmony to others and thus attract many relationships with a harmonious voice and personality. The individual wants to spend more time enhancing personal attractiveness, especially if the native is female. Hair color and appearance may be changed.

Venus in the Second House

There will be a great deal of interest in financial affairs and earning potential. The individual will spend more time with investments, personal possessions, and matters related to art, music, and entertainment. This is an ideal time to invest money and not to overspend.

The urge to spend will be strong at this time and the individual must be advised that spending should be on a small scale with savings a priority. Thus, in a future year, when this planet falls in the seventh house of the native, there will be funds to spend on others who are important to the native.

Venus in the Third House

This denotes the gracious communicator. The native is able to charm others with the ability to talk his/her way into or out of any situation. The individual will find communication and public speaking more enjoyable because of a charming manner and delivery.

There will be a tendency to overspend on travel, books, magazines, periodicals, and literature, but there will be enjoyment connected with this indulgence. This is a good time to communicate and enjoy socializing with relatives, which may not have been the case in the past.

Venus in the Fourth House

There will be more social activity in the home with this placement—parties and more social interaction with others. The home could be the place for wedding receptions, parties for politicians, birthdays, and other forms of entertainment. The individual will enjoy home decorating at this time and spend much more time at the home. This can be the person without a home of his/her own in the past. Now is the time to purchase a home—not a house for investment, but a home.

Although the individual may be one who brings a lover home, it is more likely that many people will come into the home to socialize during the year. Other individuals should be advised to accept any invitations to parties given by the native, as they will be elaborate and bring pleasure, balance, and harmony to all who attend.

Venus in the Fifth House

There will be more activity with respect to love, children, entertainment, and other pleasures. This position is mainly for the native's own indulgences rather than for a lover or children. The native will wish to bring happiness to himself or herself, probably because of previously being denied happiness. Often this indicates individuals who constantly gave of themselves and never received anything in return. Now the native will receive more gifts and pleasures. The native should be advised, however, to be moderate and not to overindulge in earthly pleasures at this time, while enjoying what is received in the way of social invitations. For the most part, this placement is mostly to bring the native happiness and balance.

Speculation with this placement should be on a small scale. It is an appropriate time to learn about speculative ventures such as stocks and bonds, since there is always a need to invest and save wisely. At this time, the individual becomes involved with friends who are actors, sports figures, entertainers, musicians, and other persons and celebrities even though the native did not seek them.

Venus in the Sixth House

It is the year to balance the system with respect to health. This is the planet of balance and the individual wishes to spend more time taking care of self. The native will be involved in social events in which alternative healing, herb remedies and bodily functions are discussed. It would be enjoyable and harmonious for the individual to be involved in health matters at this time. The native will learn to balance health and environment in order to realize not to overdo indulgences, and will enjoy working on his/her health with exercise, proper diet and learning about health.

The native now enjoys work more than in the past, with more harmony among the workforce. The individual will find there are similar interests with others at the place of employment. There will be more socializing with other employees, thus balancing out isolation at work.

Venus in the Seventh House

This is home for this planet and it doubles the effect it has on individuals. They have a tendency to overdo the social life, especially with many people in public places, almost to the point where they begin to feel tired of these activities. It would be better for the individual to work with the public instead, so that there would be a financial benefit of some kind coming to the individual. Because of extensive socializing away from home, the individual will wish to spend more time at home. This is a good time for the single person to marry or to live with another person, for this is the house of marriage and partnerships. If the individual is married, he or she will find the partner involved with many social activities throughout the solar year. The native will be charming with others and it would take no effort to achieve attention.

It is an appropriate time for legal affairs as long as it is on a small scale. It would not benefit the individual to pursue criminal or federal court actions at this time. The individual could, however, end up in court with this placement, and if the matter involves litigation on a small scale, it would turn out well for the person.

Venus in the Eighth House
This is a planetary placement that can make this a fun house. It is an intense house position for this shy and balanced planet. The individual will have sex far more often, and with renewed vitality through deep emotional and somewhat intense sexual affairs that must be faced. Life is balanced by trying a variety of sex acts, and these experiences bring joy and fun. Socializing and communication will involve sex in some way throughout the year. The intensity of this house, however, is mitigated by this planet so that sexual activities do not become so powerfully physical.

This is a good position to have if the native wishes to marry, or for the person who wishes to begin a sex life.

Psychic matters will involve socializing with those in metaphysical centers or an involvement with a psychic person. There is a strong possibility that the individual will receive a small inheritance, or benefit through a spouse or financial institution. With this planet, money will always be on a small scale as it is the source for balance. It reveals the charming socializer and it prefers to bring enjoyment and beauty to the native.

Venus in the Ninth House

There is a desire to be back in college or to travel with this placement. When there is that urge to travel, the native will have the money necessary to make the trip. It will be for fun and with friends, and not necessarily to enhance one's studies or career. This is the time for the individual to join a singles club, and to socialize with foreigners and with those in the educational field, religious organizations, philosophical groups, or in politics. These persons will find the native interesting and charming. It is truly a fun position.

The college student should be advised not to overdo social activities to a point that it affects one's studies. The energy level is high and the student is free and away from home. This is a placement that is found frequently with college students, especially the first two years at college.

Venus in the Tenth House

There is an interest in career but not necessarily any type of advancement. The native will find government interesting and may study the laws or constitution of governments around the world. There will be considerable socializing with respect to the career in that the individual could be appointed to set up social events for the government or employer.

It will be necessary to socialize to a greater extent in order to benefit the career. Now is the time for the native to socialize with superiors so that commitments can be given with respect to career advancement. It will not necessarily be an activity that the individual will enjoy, but after many years of employment, it will be good for the native to socialize with those in authority.

This is also a placement that could involve the individual, single or married, in an affair with someone in authority or another employee in the workplace.

Venus in the Eleventh House

With this placement there is an enjoyment of friends. This includes many social activities with those with whom the native previously had no opportunity to socialize. This can be the person who was married for many years and is now free to socialize with anyone. A friend could become a lover during the solar year. This is a frivolous and fun position and a time to make friends and promote relationships, as this is a joyful house for this planet.

It is a time to join clubs if the native is unmarried, or to join social clubs catering to married couples. This is a good year to join an organization in order to make new friends and be a part of society that was impossible to join in the past. The individual may be asked to join an organization, and should accept. The individual may wish to help a group monetarily or through acceptance of a position as an officer. An organization is a good place for the native to socialize and exhibit a charming manner.

Venus in the Twelfth House

There can be difficulties with this placement. The individual could easily make improper friendships at this time. There is a great possibility for the individual to be involved with alcohol and drugs, and to socialize with the wrong element of society. The native could socialize with enemies, the very people who wish to harm to him or her. The native will be more outgoing and social at this time and thus easily attract the wrong type of person.

There will be a tendency to overspend by indulging in drugs or alcohol. The native should be very careful with this placement because he or she will not realize the trouble being invited with the lower types. It can bring depression and fear requiring treatment by professionals when this position is used improperly.

A more positive activity for the native would be to socialize at a higher, more spiritual level. This is a very spiritual position if the individual chooses to remain on a high level. It brings out one's charitable and generous side. The individual will have a desire to help the unfortunate in some way, or to volunteer time in a hospital or institution. This is the house of secrets and seclusion, and in order for the individual to balance this placement it must be done through charity and compassion for the unfortunate on one side of the scale, and through various forms of creativity and artistic endeavors on the other side of the scale.

Depending on the seriousness of the illness, the individual will not be harmed or have something detrimental occur while confined to a hospital. It is not necessarily an unfortunate position for hospitalization. This may not be true if confinement is necessary in a mental institution. However, the person will find it necessary to spend a little money on medication to keep the system in balance.

This is a placement where the individual can be involved with the wrong person, who influences the individual into a situation not of his or her own choosing. For example, the person may have an affair and then be in a position to have to keep it secret. This planet is the charming socializer and when an individual socializes in places where alcohol and drugs are available, there could be involvement in secret affairs, including making money on a small scale through illegal means. This is a position that is often found in the natal charts of criminals and swindlers, and although this type of activity may be unintentional during a solar return year, it could definitely occur.

Mercury—The Communicator

It is the planet that brings an awareness, an awakening, like a light bulb bringing light into a room, especially if it conjuncts another planet in the chart or conjuncts a planet by progression.

Mercury in the First House

A higher intelligence is indicated with this placement. It gives the individual the ability to convey exactly what points he or she is attempting to communicate to others. The individual will have the ability to grasp information easily and readily, together with an ability to teach and explain knowledge. This is the year the individual develops a quick wit and a charming personality. An individual who was not necessarily quick-witted in the past will now have a burst of mental energy as he or she will have many causes and events to deal with throughout the solar year. There will be communication with respect to travel, relatives, and neighbors.

At this time there is a connection between the person's spirituality, mental outlook, and the environment. The individual should be advised not to begin a project that cannot be completed or that the individual has no intention of finishing; it will work against the native in some way. This is an enlightening position irrespective of the sign placement, and an excellent placement overall.

Mercury in the Second House

Communication will involve money and financial affairs. The mind of the person will be more on money than at other times in the past. Worries will involve money and the financial situation. The native now realizes that more time should have been spent in taking care of money matters. It is a good position for investments and for signing contracts involving financial matters.

This is not the indicator of one who spends money on travel. It is one who will discuss the expense of taking a trip but who will not necessarily take the trip. The individual may discuss the purchase of an automobile, but not actually make the purchase. This placement has more to do with the signing of contracts for investment or financial gain, such as social events for profit, the arts and crafts, or other types of investments. This is a placement that pertains more than any other time to the personal affairs of the individual—physically, mentally and spiritually.

Mercury in the Third House

This intensifies communication—communication just to communicate. There is a tendency to talk and communicate extensively. However, it is an opportunity for the individual to pass on knowledge to others. It is an ideal placement for one who is in a teaching capacity as there will be the ability to simplify the material and make it easier for others to understand what is being discussed. It is a good year to write articles for publication in magazines, such as articles involving travel, relatives, neighborhoods, and the communication industry.

Although the individual will discuss travel plans and probably take a trip during the year, more will be spent on travel for the purpose of visiting relatives. Travel can pertain to a symposium or for study in a particular area, but for the most part, this placement is best used in writing articles for publication even though it may be for small organizational newsletters. The articles will be positive and well received.

Mercury in the Fourth House
The placement indicates an individual who will whine about something during the solar year. Except for matters of this house, the native will tend to be a little more lazy pertaining to other areas of life. The individual will spend more time around the home, have more conversations with family, become involved in real estate, or simply be more domestic. This is the placement of the couch potato; the native will want to spend more time around the house.

The person does have the desire to communicate outside of the home area and can be involved in writing contracts or operating a business pertaining to communication out of the home. This is a good placement for one who has a computer at home and wishes to communicate with others around the world via the Internet.

It must be stressed that this placement is the indicator of one who will whine and exhibit a moody disposition—up one minute and down the next. The individual will be moody, emotional, and changeable. If there is a dominant parent involved, the native will whine to the parent. The mental state will be volatile during the solar year. It is best that the individual take out frustrations on the computer.

Mercury in the Fifth House

This indicates the positive and fun person with an ample supply of vitality. The individual will wish to speculate, have a good time, and socialize. The mind is set on love, romance, speculation, amusements, and entertainment.

There will be a good rapport with children during this solar year. The personality will be positive and outgoing, and the native will wish to have a good time without worry of any kind. This is a good position for the person who had a miserable year previously, as this fortunate placement is needed. Misery is something an individual brings to oneself, for the way one thinks is the way one feels.

Mercury in the Sixth House

This is the constant complainer, such as the hypochondriac. The individual will espouse the wonders of herbs for health and the benefits received by using herbs for healing. This depends on the individual. Those who have had a very negative outlook throughout life or who are preoccupied with alcohol and drugs would not particularly care about herbal remedies.

This is an either-or placement. The individual will worry about work, health, pets, or the employer and employees, or the person will take a much more positive role by focusing on natural products for health, being dutiful at work, taking care of pets and animals, and being helpful to other employees in the workplace. Either way, it is good for communicating what has been learned about natural healing.

A person who is in bad health could use this position to successfully cure any health problem by researching and using natural remedies that personal research has shown to be beneficial.

Mercury in the Seventh House

There will be considerable involvement with the public and considerable discussions with the partner, laws, or social issues. The native will be before the public in some capacity, whether lecturing, writing, or communicating in some way. The individual will be called upon to relay some type of information to others, whether by word of mouth, through an article, or through the Internet. This is a given and will definitely occur.

The individual will be able to understand all types of contracts because he or she has done the necessary homework to gain the knowledge. The native will be considered an expert on contracts, and if anyone wishes to have a pending contract reviewed, this is the person that should be consulted. The native, whether or not an attorney, will be very much prepared before appearing in court.

Mercury in the Eighth House

This is a very interesting placement in that it brings about a psychic experience in some way. The native will see it, communicate it, or have it in a dream state or while engaged in sex. It is a cycle returning approximately every eight years.

The person will have a type of psychic experience not experienced in the past. Those who are already psychic, will find there is a demand for that ability as they now will be able to better communicate psychic talents. The individual that has this placement naturally and now has it also in the solar return chart will give many more psychic readings, lecture on psychic matters, and communicate their talents for the benefit of many people.

Sex, death, inheritance, taxes, research and insurance will be uppermost in the mind and will be something that must be dealt with during the solar year. This is not an easy placement for the individual to handle without spiritual guidance. The individual will dwell on death not only with respect to self, but also with respect to those who are close.

It must be emphasized that with this placement it is the psychic that is the most important, especially as human beings enter the new age. Those who have never believed nor ever had psychic experiences will begin to awaken, for they will become more spiritually aware with psychic ability. The native must be told to prepare for a psychic experience and not to be afraid. In most cases, however, the experience will have already occurred.

Mercury in the Ninth House

The mind focuses on philosophy, foreign lands and people, long distance travel, higher education, and religion, and the individual will be able to discuss any or all of these subjects with anyone. The individual who works in publishing or in a professional capacity this solar year will do very well. The native will be called upon to lecture, especially if in a college environment. On a higher scale, the native can speak before a publication-related or professional group.

This is the year the individual becomes involved in spiritual matters and takes on a greater understanding of spiritual awareness. Concepts and ideologies previously accepted as truths are no longer valid to the native, who now will wish to do more research to find spiritual truths.

The college student with this position should be told that he or she can become too knowledgeable and egotistical and thus have difficulty with professors. This is not the time to lecture professors. This placement is very good for expressing opinions and for communicating, writing, and getting articles published. It is a positive placement and a very good position overall.

Mercury in the Tenth House

It is generally a poor placement unless the career is in the communications field: teaching, writing, publishing, working for a government agency, sales and advertising, or dealing with the poor and unfortunate. If the career of the individual is not in these fields of endeavor, it would not prove to be a beneficial placement.

It can benefit the individual involved with the government in some way on a short term basis through a contract obtained by the individual's company. Or it can be the whistleblower if the person is so inclined, or it can be one who advises the government with respect to a certain project or activity.

For the most part, most people prefer not to hear from the government, but with this position the person will receive communication from a city, county, state, or federal government agency. This can be from the Internal Revenue Service, from a municipal agency notifying the native of an unpaid traffic fine, or something that involves property. For the most part, the incidents would be brief and not necessarily very pleasant.

Mercury in the Eleventh House

This is an excellent position for expressing oneself, either with friends or in writing and other communications for extra income. It would not provide major income, but only small amounts through communication ability or ideas that would benefit a certain group or organization. Income can also come through writing on scientific subjects.

Primarily, however, the individual will spend more time communicating and socializing with friends or traveling with friends or an organization. Seeking an increase in salary is advisable at this time if there are good aspects to this placement. It will be an easy year for the individual.

Mercury in the Twelfth House

The native will have an inspiring outlook for the year through spirit sources. Psychic gifts can be used to write music or to communicate with entities on a higher plane, or it can be one with an evil mind. This is an either-or placement in that the individual will be concerned with drugs and alcohol and the evil side of life, and yet still be involved to benefit a hospital in some way, lecture on certain diseases, or work at fund raising for a good cause. It will fluctuate between the two. The individual will be inspired by a psychic gift one day, and the next be talking trash at the local bar. The person could get high on drugs and become inspired, or the person could inspire others. The individual should be advised to try to develop his or her psychic gifts, but to do this only if there has been some experience with the psychic in the past.

Moon—The Illuminator of the Soul

The Moon gives individuals the ability to look into the soul. This can cause the person to become very emotional and changeable for the solar year. The year can be highly emotional if the person is troubled, or through positive soul searching, there can be illumination. To some, it can be handled in a delicate manner; to others it can cause a great heartache. It will be a year of soul searching wherever located in the solar return chart.

The Moon should be progressed throughout the year. Using an ephemeris to determine its twenty-four hour motion, subtract its position on the day of the solar return from the following day. The daily motion of its degrees and minutes is then divided by twelve to arrive at its monthly progression. The progressed aspects of the Moon to planets in the solar return chart must be kept within an orb of one degree, applying or leaving.

Moon in the First House

The individual will be self-oriented, doing things for self rather than being concerned about others. The native can become emotional about life, as well as influences of females and the home. There will be emotional upheavals as well as emotional respites. The native will spend much of the time dealing with self.

This is the year the individual will take the time to study his or her early childhood to discover why certain emotional problems exist. If the person is troubled, this would be a good time to go into therapy to work out the problems. This is a very good position for soul searching and for self-development. Negatively, it will be the person who achieves little or no illumination during the course of the year. Individuals should be advised to try to focus on why they are the way they are, as this is a good year to learn about themselves.

If the native is a male, this can bring a type of feminine personality to the individual, and thus males could attract more females. It is also a good time for men to learn about their female side. The native will be much more involved with women or could deal with affairs of women, including the mother.

Moon in the Second House

The individual will become quite emotional and changeable with respect to the financial situation, which can be very detrimental or very beneficial. They can become too emotional over resources and thus lose financially in some way. There will be an urge to spend too much money on women or on feminine things if poorly aspected to Mars, or conflicts over the financial condition with the partner that would increase indebtedness.

The individual will spend time soul searching with respect to the emotional side in dealing with finances. No dramatic changes should be made in the financial situation at this time.

Unless all aspects to this position are positive, this would not be the time to make a very large purchase, such as a home, because emotions would cause the native to spend too much money. It will be a time when the individual will soul search financial affairs and emotions. For those who have very little interest in financial affairs, it will be a conscious soul search to learn their beliefs on this subject.

Moon in the Third House

The person will be flighty at this time, finding it difficult to sleep because of being pulled in many directions emotionally. There will be involvement with relatives and in numerous short travels. This is the year the native will soul search his/her own and family history. The native will evaluate the family and how he or she fits in the family structure.

This is a good year for the person to realize how he or she feels about relatives. If the individual does not have any relatives, he or she will become emotional over the fact there are no relatives and will try to find someone who could be considered a relative. Poor aspects to this placement can bring about arguments and difficulties with relatives.

This is a good year for soul-searching and reflection, but it is not a good year for lecturing or study. However, it would be an advantageous period for the person to lecture on emotional problem, feminine affairs, Moon changes; and soul searching. It is not a good year for health if the individual is getting too little sleep and thus becomes nervous and frustrated over projects that cannot be completed.

Moon in the Fourth House

This is not a desirable placement. It reveals much soul-searching with respect to self, home, the end of Earth life, the dominant parent, and all other matters of this house. The native will become emotional over the past and what it has brought. The emotions can involve a lost relationship with a female who was important. The person should stay away from the kitchen as much as possible as he or she will eat far too much due to emotional issues.

Only a negligible amount of time will be spent outside the home. If the native continues to spend all his or her time homebound, then the individual should be advised to use this solar year in some type of construction that can improve the home base. In any event, this is a placement indicating a change either within the home or a complete change of residence, Emotional upsets can include the loss of a dominant parent or anything involving the home. The sign cusp ruled by Cancer can indicate the kind of change that will take place.

Moon in the Fifth House

This is a nice placement to have for the solar year. Individuals will fall in love easily and will be very emotional over their love affairs. This is the house of fun and entertainment, which also includes sex for fun: sex with many others or simply different types of sex with one person.

There will be a period during which the individual will soul-search regarding why past relationships were not successful; as a result, an attempt will be made to improve a present relationship.

This will be a happy time as the native will take on a childlike quality and become changeable like a child. It will be a good year for making friends as well as being involved with female relatives. This is an appropriate time to be involved with female activities or any activity that would include children. The solar year will find the native in love with love.

Long term investments are not recommended due to the emotional and changeable nature of this placement. Emotions will cause the person to take undue risks in investing. Overall, however, it will be an enjoyable year and the individual should take the time to enjoy it because the Moon could be in the fourth house the following year.

Moon in the Sixth House

This is a good position for work, pets, and health, and individuals will expend much activity and energy in these affairs. There will be soul-searching with respect to these matters for they will enjoy them more at this time. The native will find that work is enjoyable and that it is somewhat like a home away from home.

Although emotions will run up and down with respect to health and other areas related to this house, particularly if there is a poor aspect involving Saturn or another heavy planet, it is not an unfortunate position. This can be the person who will soul-search about health and work in the context of changing bad habits and incorporate new and better ones. The location of a health problem can be determined by the decanate of the sign on the cusp of this house.

Since this is the energy of change, a job change is possible, and it may not be the individual's decision. This can be determined by looking to the tenth house and its ruler.

These people can find themselves in an environment dealing with women, female affairs, or a new house. With this position, the person will become involved in all affairs of this house in one capacity or another.

It is a good time for introspection for this is the placement for reflecting on self through soul searching. This placement in the first six houses of the chart will definitely bring this about.

Moon in the Seventh House
Natives will find themselves before the public or working for the public. They may become emotional about it, but in one way or the other they will be in the public eye for it will draw them to public affairs. It will be a very dynamic year for the person. The native could work for female causes and for the good of the public. If poorly aspected, it would affect the native emotionally in a negative way, but overall the individual will be able to handle it.

This is a good placement for a marriage proposal or to be married if this was contemplated prior to the solar return year. It will also be soul searching with respect to the partner and the native may wish to do something about that situation. The individual can become emotional over the partner or the partner can become emotional over the individual. The person will reflect to others what is seen in them. It all has to do with the native being before the public because of changes that are made or in some other capacity.

Litigation with this placement will be changeable because the individual will be changeable. The native will flip-flop in making decisions. This is not a good position for court room involvement. It would be better for the partner to appear in court of the native.

Moon in the Eighth House
This is a good position for soul-searching. There will be many psychic experiences similar to Mercury in this house, as well as unusual and unexpected psychic occurrences in addition to very emotional sexual encounters. Emotions will involve all matters of this house, such as insurance, inheritance, other people's or the partner's money, death, crime, and the underworld. It can cause the individual to be dependent on another or bring about a very emotional time in dealing with the affairs of the dead and the psychic. The individual will have the experience of seeing ghosts at

this time and can become frightened if there has been no background in such experiences. It is an appropriate time for the native to seek spiritual guidance as one could easily be pulled in the wrong direction with this placement. The soul must be guarded at this time as it can be overtaken by evil sources.

Sex will be emotional and intense. Poorly aspected, it could be one who would enjoy the negative side of sex, even to the point of abusing the partner to achieve sexual excitement. The native can be drawn into dark areas if this position is not well aspected. It is a position where the individual needs to be careful with anyone with whom they are involved. A sexual commitment can lead the individual in the wrong direction. This is a placement that can be very binding, and blinding, with respect to an emotional sexual relationship. It is a position that needs good aspects of the Sun and Mercury to enable the person to handle it favorably. A poor aspect of Saturn or Pluto, especially Pluto, could place the person in a dangerous position.

Surgery is ruled by this house and there is the possibility of a major or minor surgical procedure. Aspects to the twelfth house of illness and hospitalization could determine the seriousness and outcome of the problem. But for all intents and purposes, this can be a very intense spiritual awakening or a very emotional and intense sexual experience. It will be a dynamic placement for the year; therefore, it would be wise to monitor it closely throughout the year. It is the time the individual searches the soul with respect to many things in life, especially all matters of this house.

Moon in the Ninth House
This is the house of long journeys, foreign travel, higher education, publishing, the spiritual, philosophy, and religion. Although not a strong placement, it does give the individual a spiritual uplift. The native will feel good, positive, and have a very good year. It is a good position for the person who is involved in travel of some kind, and it is good for travel with women or over bodies of water. The person could be inclined to travel by the course of the Moon. It

is a fine position for learning and to reflect on spiritual destiny through soul searching. The individual at this time should soul search to discover true spiritual values. The other side of this is the person who decides to go off the deep end and travel to faraway lands to search for the soul through a foreign religion or philosophy.

A journey is possible at this time because of a prior commitment or because of a situation arising that would necessitate the trip. The changeability of this energy can also affect those who are in a course of study that can cause them to change courses or profession. Aspects to this placement will determine whether the changes will be favorable or unfortunate. The person should be advised not to make any changes until after the end of the solar return year if at all possible.

Moon in the Tenth House

This is not a desirable placement. It brings difficulty throughout the year. Individuals will feel they are being drawn in all directions, especially with respect to career. This is the time for the person to soul-search with respect to career choices.

It greatly involves the older individual because of its unsettling effect, which causes instability. This can be someone who has an emotional dependence on government, if in the latter years of life. It is a difficult position for the elderly, requiring much support from friends and relatives. Younger persons are not as subject to the pull in many directions as the elderly; however, they will feel that older persons are always picking on them and will tend to rebel.

This is the time the individual will need friends and relatives for support. One could become very unsettled as it will be a painful year. It is a blessing that it is only for the solar year and that the experiences can be overcome. This can involve problems with those in authority that affects the career or changes in the organization that can cause emotional stress. The native will feel that the time has come to make a change. With good aspects to Saturn and the heavy planets, it will be the year to make the change.

Moon in the Eleventh House

This is a good placement for the solar return year. The person will have a very happy and fun year, achieving many hopes and wishes. It is a time to find little sources of income that were unavailable in prior years. The native is given this blessing because he or she has worked hard and successfully up to this solar year and has been rewarded with some fun and happiness. There could be travel with an organization and the enjoyment of friends. It is the time for soul searching with respect to their life and how it has been good.

There will be an increase in income as the person is under a lucky cycle. If an increase in salary does not come about, this is a good time to ask for an increase.

Moon in the Twelfth House

This is not a poor placement. It is the person who decides to look deep within the soul and thus change what he or she does not like. It is a good time to realize dark secrets and what has been kept hidden from self and others. If it is necessary, this is a good time for counseling in order to develop abilities. The native will see him/herself for what he or she really is, and also see others for what they are. The native may not like what is seen, but this is the time for awareness. This is a very good position to gain through karmic experiences and thus elevate the soul for the next incarnation.

The individual will see things about which he or she was previously unaware. The native will see himself or herself as the enemy, and what he or she has done to self, as well as those who have been secret enemies throughout his/her life. This is the time for introspection. The individual can choose to ignore what is seen, but more often than not the person with this position can truly become aware of self and become frightened enough to want to change. It is the person who is truly inspired by this placement.

This is an appropriate time to study psychology or psychic development, for it is definitely a time when the person will experience self- awareness through interpretation of one's own dreams. This is a way in which spirit sources try to get individuals to understand themselves. However, there are always those who do not choose to pay attention to what they see. Therefore, they will miss the opportunity to advance the soul. This is a karmic position one can choose to accept in a positive way, or to ignore this blessing and go into seclusion and depression.

The individual should be advised to always search for the positive even though one is looking within and finding those things he or she dislikes, there is no resined to remain that way. This placement is only for the year; but it is a year when the individual can make great karmic advances in life. It is a time to grow and develop. No one is given more than they can be handled in an incarnation.

The Progression of the Moon

When the Moon progresses out of one house and into the next during the course of the solar return, it will continue to activate the house of its original position. Watch for other aspects being formed that could be a way out of a difficult aspect or it can be just the opposite, thus bringing about unfortunate results. Check the progression of the Moon and its aspects as the year unfolds keeping a very tight orb of one degree either applying or separating .

The position of the Sun and Moon and aspects will disclose almost all one needs to know about the solar year.

Mars—The Great Energizer

Mars is the planet that brings great energy in many forms. It is usually quick energy that brings great activity to its house placement; however, it ultimately creates a loss of interest there. It represents conflicts, when it is poorly aspected, and confrontations even under good aspects.

Mars in the First House

The individual develops a hot temper with this placement in addition to a feeling of warmth throughout the body, and is much more energetic throughout the year. It is a burst of energy for the native but at the same time the energy is depleted as a lot of heat and emotional and mental energy is dissipated. The person will be more argumentative toward others than in previous years.

Those individuals who tend to avoid expressing themselves and who are not outspoken will become far more expressive and argumentative at this time. They should be much more assertive during the year and should not try to hold back this high output of energy. This is a necessary position for the person who needs spurts of energy to carry out activities.

Mars in the Second House

Energy is devoted to financial affairs and possessions. The native will go through resources rather rapidly and later be disgruntled with the situation that was caused by rash decisions. He or she should be warned to avoid rash decisions with respect to finances, for in the haste to make investments, money will be lost.

Used in a positive way, the native should try to improve upon what he or she already possesses. In this way, conflicts or arguments over resources and possessions will be avoided. This is not the year to overspend. It is a placement that could bring about a loss of money. However, if this planet is in a grand trine it will bring some quick money to the individual.

Mars in the Third House

The individual will spend a great deal of time communicating. There will also be problems connected with relatives, neighbors, peers, or short journeys. This is the time for minor traffic accidents and the person should be advised not to travel in heavy traffic if this placement is not well aspected. Conflicts are certain with all matters of this house. The energy of this planet highly excites but does not remain for any length of time.

This can indicate an accident involving a relative or the person who develops a hot temper while in traffic, thus causing an accident. The incidents are brought about quickly but end quickly.

Mars in the Fourth House

There will be a great deal of activity with respect to the affairs of this house. There will be arguments in the home and the person will not want to spend much time in the home, simply rushing in and rushing out. If the individual is living with parents, it is an opportune time to leave, if desired, although one should not be in a great hurry and should use care in finding a new residence.

The home will be more stressful than at other times in the past, as it will not be a place for relaxation. There is a lot of rapid energy with this position, but the individual should be advised not to sell the home at this time.

Fire and accidents can occur with this placement, which would be caused by the individuals themselves due to their haste and lack of attention. It is a time to be careful around the home and with those affairs involving the home.

To use this placement in a positive manner, the individual should use physical energy in construction of something related to the home. It is an opportune year for those who wish to go into the restaurant business or to be involved in cooking in some way. This would be using this placement in a constructive and positive manner.

Mars in the Fifth House

There will be a great deal of activity with respect to entertainment, children, love, and romance. The tendency will be to rush into a love relationship, only to have it burn out later. This is a position somewhat like having Venus in Aries.

The person will want to invest in something or go on a gambling junket. Money will leave rapidly or come rapidly. It is similar to its placement in the second house. Either way, it does not remain in effect for any length of time. If this position is well aspected to Jupiter and Venus, it can be a good time to make an investment of some kind, or to make an investment ruled by a sign that is in a grand trine. With a grand trine and with no negative aspects, an investment can be made.

This placement has more to do with having a good time than it does a concern about investments. The person will fall in love, go out on the town, and be more concerned with pleasure. This is a placement of sex for fun, entertainment, and self-satisfaction. It is not a year for a long and steady love relationship. With respect to young children, parents should be aware that they can become involved in some type of incident, or accident, during the solar year.

The individual will likely attend sporting events, as there will be an interest in this activity, but one will not necessarily physically engage in sports. The natal chart will indicate those who will be physically involved in sports.

Mars in the Sixth House
The individual will spend a great deal of time and energy with respect to the place of employment, easily becoming angry with other employees or those in authority. Frustrations and irritations will be taken out on pets or other small animals. The individual could become highly charged at work, but at the same time burn out just as quickly.

This indicates one who will have a problem with health, but it will be only a temporary flare-up such as a fever or aches and pains, or it can be one who is just sick of having to go to work each day.

This is not the time for the eligible individual to join the military. It will be a whim that can cost the person greatly. The native will enjoy being in a military environment for a time, but that joy will be short lived. It will then be next to impossible to leave. This is an opportune time to start a long term project, because it will bring many benefits at a future time.

Mars in the Seventh House

The energy is in finding a partner, whether it is a new partner, an old partner, or revitalizing an old love. However, it is not an ideal time to be married even though the person spends a great deal cf time pursuing a partner. Rushing into a partnership will result in disappointment for the individual or the individual will disappoint the partner.

Neither is it a good time for litigation, as it would not work out in one's best interest. The native should not enter into any lawsuits because it would be a short term event with a negative outcome, unless this position is very well aspected. If the individual is an attorney or a judge, he or she would find fresh enthusiasm towards the courtroom and the chosen career.

This is the time the person can be misunderstood and at times considered overbearing, or domineering, especially in close relationships. It affects personal relationships and partnerships rather than business partnerships. Business partnerships are generally formed by contractual agreements, mutually agreed upon, that guides the partnership.

Overall, it is the year the native will be before the public, involved in social events, or in the courtroom either as an observer, witness, juror, plaintiff, defendant, or for other reasons.

Mars in the Eighth House

There will be a great deal of energy involving sexual pursuits, and activities will be more on a personal level. The native will enjoy sex more than in the past. At this time, individuals can get in over their heads, or in arguments, over a sexual relationship. This can also involve other people's money, taxes, insurance, inheritance, criminal activity, or the occult. If the person is not pursuing a career in these areas, then the interest will be in sex or the occult. The individual develops an interest in the occult but finds that the interest is only for a brief period of time. It is a temporary phase; one gets into it hastily and then the interest fades.

This is the year the native hears about a death, but this placement does not involve the individual's own death. There will be involvement with affairs connected to a death, such as insurance or the cemetery. This placement involves the individual in a deep sexual relationship which can be easily mistaken for true love. For the most part, these persons simply need to express themselves through sex.

Mars in the Ninth House
The individual jumps into philosophical matters; or changes their career pursuits in college. The native will spend a great deal of time involved with colleges or with college affairs, travel, or become embroiled in arguments with all the matters of this house.

The energy of the planet is softened in this house and therefore it is not really a poor position for the year. The individual can debate the philosophies of life, which will be quite enjoyable. The vocabulary increases and the native uses all the words he or she knows to express knowledge, especially with respect to education, philosophy, religion, foreign countries, and travel. Others will consider the individual to be a know-it-all and thus form resentments. In keeping with the action of this planet, however, the resentments will be short lived.

It is advisable that the individual use care in making travel arrangements, for this is not a good year for distant travels unless there are very good aspects to this position. If the individual decides to make a long journey anyway, the stay at any one place will not be long.

Mars in the Tenth House
This is not an exciting position for this planet. There will be a greater interest in career and the government, and more energy in all matters of this house, which will be quite stressful. This is not a good time to try to change careers because desire could prompt premature action. No changes should be made at this time unless there is a conjunction or trine to Uranus.

There will be arguments with others in the workplace, which could be very detrimental and cause termination. The native could divulge certain things that should be left dormant causing difficulties with superiors and immediate termination. This placement causes the individual to use poor judgement in matters of career. It is also not a good time to become embroiled in arguments with law enforcement officers, superiors, or government officials.

Termination can result because of the downsizing of a business; the loss of a government contract, or other such reasons. This is the year that the individual should do his/her very best in career and work areas because what is done at this time can bring many benefits and recognition at a later time.

Mars in the Eleventh House

This is a very interesting position because the individual will spend a great deal of time with friends and in heavy pursuit of good times with organizational activities. There will be a great interest in these affairs. If the position is not well aspected, the native will be more argumentative with friends or cause problems for an organization.

This is the time the individual will want to find an activity that will bring extra income, but that interest burns out quickly. It will be something the native finds stimulating and exciting, the ver thing that is quickly lost.

With this planet, there is a loss of interest after a short space of time. The person jumps into something at full speed; then reality sets in and the idea and excitement burns out. For all practical purposes, this will be the individual whose energy will be expended to increase income and to realize hopes and wishes.

Mars in the Twelfth House

Although this can indicate surgery, it really brings an interest in affairs of this house, such as drugs, alcohol, disease, hospitals, institutions, prisons, secret enemies, and the psychic mind. This is the year the individual confronts secret enemies, which is not advisable. The native should be advised to refrain from confronting or arguing with a secret enemy and to stay away from institutions of all kinds.

The person has a fascination in helping others by volunteering or working in a hospital, but the interest is only brief. The native will not like working in a hospital or institution.

This is a very complex position and depends on the character of the person and what is done for a living. If the person is a criminal, he or she certainly would not volunteer to work in a hospital helping others. This is a position where the individual joins an organization or hospital to help others in some way, but then finds it too stressful or uncomfortable and wishes to leave. The initial interest eventually wanes.

Psychic flashes will be experienced but will not remain. There will be brilliant psychic flashes that appear like dreams, but the individual will not remember them. There will be an interest in psychic affairs, but the interest will be of a short duration. The energies will come and go, although when a fixed sign is involved, the interest will remain a bit longer.

Because of emotional upsets, the individual can go into seclusion. To offset this, the person should pursue the research of any subject of interest, such as the paranormal, the unknown, astrology, ancient history, extraterrestrials, or anything that is very old. This will provide them an uplift and enhance the ego.

Jupiter—Provider of Abundance and Knowledge

The beneficial one. This is expansion, happiness, joyfulness, enrichment, the provider of abundance and wealth of knowledge. In short, it is known as the benefic planet, with beauty and benefits combined. Most of the placements of this planet are there as a benefit to help the native undo an unpleasant past experience.

Jupiter in the First House

The sign and house of the natal chart that bears the sign of the Ascendant of the solar return shows where the individual will be fortunate throughout the year. It brings good fortune to the person who had an unfortunate previous year, such as Saturn in the first house. It denotes one who has been through a very difficult ordeal—and this is a blessing to help the individual realize that the ordeal was not necessarily a burden.

This placement helps the native out of financial difficulties and there will be a great deal of luck not experienced previously. Unusual benefits to come during the year, not necessarily lottery winnings, but something unexpected and beneficial.

The individual will have a much happier outlook on life and look on the bright side instead of the negative side of things. The attitude will be positive for the year.

Jupiter in the Second House

The native will be inclined to spend on material things, and it would be a beneficial time to deal with financial institutions. The native should be advised not to overspend, as there will be a compulsion to spend freely. Control of spending could be determined by the natal chart.

There will be sufficient funds flowing to the person because of need to recover financially from a previous solar return. This position is brought to the native to overcome an unpleasant experience in a prior year. The person would need to have something to assist through a very difficult financial event.

From the opposite house, benefits could come from insurance during the year or through a future solar return.

Jupiter in the Third House

Spiritual communication will be beneficial at this time. The person will be drawn to the study of philosophy and spiritual matters. It will be helpful for those who had difficulty in staying true to their ideology and faith. The placement is necessary for them in order that they once again can see the spiritual side of life, especially if their spirituality was shaken in a prior year.

There will be benefits through short trips and it will bring some contacts with relatives, but this would be minor. The main theme of this placement is dealing with spiritual matters, with all other areas of this house being secondary. It is spiritual and philosophical communication because there is a need for it at this time. The native has undergone a difficult period in the past involving spiritual values.

Jupiter in the Fourth House

This brings happiness to the home and can bring back loved ones who have been away for a long period of time. Prior to this solar year, there would have been turmoil in the home, and this will bring happiness, warmth, spiritual matters, affluence, or even a prayer group to the home and family.

This is the time for the individual to consult a channel to contact a deceased loved one or dominant figure in order to cement a relationship that was previously not amicable.

An addition or an expansion of the home is likely, which brings joy to the individual. There will be an inner happiness as well as a creative happiness. The native will wish to stay at home, where happiness will be found during the solar year. This is a very good time to make improvements in the home, grow a garden, or beautify the home in some way. It is a joyous time for family affairs, more so than in previous years.

Jupiter in the Fifth House

Natives will find ways to amuse and enjoy themselves. This benefit is given to them because they did not have the opportunity to enjoy themselves in a prior year. They will spend much time having fun and pursuing entertainment, enjoying sports or being involved with children in some way. They will need this placement to relax for a year.

This is the house of self-expression, and the individual will express the need for a vacation type of living. It is time to enjoy life for the entire year. The native will, of course, have to continue daily routines, but will find enjoyment in sporting events, entertainment, cruises, and other things considered enjoyment. Expression is through fun.

Jupiter in the Sixth House

This is an excellent placement for health. It is needed by the person because of difficulty in the past with health and work environment. This will overcome a previous dislike of going to work each day. For example, this could be a person who changed jobs and now finds work is a benefit and joy.

Individuals with this placement will seek information about acquiring better health habits, such as joining a health spa or exercise club. This will also include pets, where the native experiences joy through pets and finds ways to improve their pets in some way. This is a good time to give a pet to an elderly individual because it would bring joy, companionship and love, thus benefitting the health.

Jupiter in the Seventh House

This is the year the native is in the public eye, or more so than in prior years. The native will seek those areas that would benefit the public, whereas in previous years the individual shied away from public life. The individual now enjoys dealing with the public. This position has more to do with the person expanding and learning how to deal with self with respect to the public. It is the year to balance and expand particular talents. If the person was out of balance previously, this is the time to bring balance to the life. It does bring joy to the partner, but this position has more to do with the public.

There will be a benefit in joining those organizations that would be of benefit to the person, or consulting law libraries at a university for knowledge and information. For the most part, this position has to do with the public, although it does help the person overcome a fear developed in the past by returning confidence with respect to partnerships and the public. It would not necessarily rectify a broken marriage, since this would be determined by the natal chart. This will restore confidence in a partner, or through a partner, but not necessarily the same partner. It will be through another person.

If a lawsuit is contemplated, this is a beneficial time to seek redress in court and, of course, it would bring the individual into the public eye.

Jupiter in the Eighth House
This is communication with the spirit world. It brings the spiritual into the psychic realm. It could be one who was a very conservative, religious individual who had nothing to do with new age matters, but now has a greater understanding, or awareness, of matters concerning the spirit world. This will also bring a greater understanding or awareness of matters concerning inheritance through insurance or legacies. The native will want to take out additional insurance at this time, and by doing so, it will ultimately benefit the person.

Joy could come to the individual through the knowledge that a deceased loved one is not suffering but is happy in spirit. This could come through a dream or through a visit in a spirit form. This will show the native, especially one who is narrow-minded about such things, that there is another world of living. It expands psychic ability, coming in the form of dreams, bringing exciting and happy dreams. It is a time of investments and affairs of the afterlife.

Although this is the house of the gambler and gambling, this solar return placement does not involve gambling but only true investing, such as the purchase of insurance annuities, bonds, and other safe investments.

Jupiter in the Ninth House

The individual becomes joyfully interested in returning to a higher study. This is not a strong placement but it does induce the person to areas of philosophy, law, spiritual matters, and to invest in the future of professional life. It restores confidence in the legal system after an unfortunate experience involving the law. It is a blessing to the person for having the character and will to have endured the experience.

Benefits come in the form of knowledge and understanding of the spirit realm, journeys, and study. The previous solar return and the natal chart reflect the legal problem and the reason the individual is enjoying this benefit.

Jupiter in the Tenth House

This brings considerable activity with the career or working with the government. It is the person who has been searching for an enjoyable career but without success. With this placement, the individual will find a new career, bringing expansion and knowledge. It will be necessary to retrain and learn new things, but the new career will bring many benefits. It is also the year to work within the government if the person is involved in this area.

This is the house of poverty, but this placement lessens the problem. Those who have been unemployed will now find less poverty and more joy through a career. This does indicate money from the government, but not be unemployment compensation or welfare. Unemployment is not the effect of this planet as it is expansive. Suffering is indicated by a Saturnian effect. It can be a subsidy of some kind, such as what farmers receive for their crops. The person will want to go back to work and not take a government handout. Work could be found within the government if desired.

Although this does not necessarily mean a career change, if the individual was contemplating s change in career, this would be a beneficial time to make the change. It will benefit the native physically and spiritually.

Jupiter in the Eleventh House

Jupiter can be very erratic in this house, but one way or another it brings goodness to the person. There will be increased income from the career. An important side to this placement is that whatever is wished for it will come true. Whenever the individual focuses on something, it occurs. It is to the benefit of the person who had a difficult time previously because of overspending on material things or organizations.

There is an erratic behavior to this planet here and the individual should be careful what is wished for. Every time something is wished for, it comes true and the native will overcompensate. After its transit in the solar return ends, the benefits or money will be no more. For example, the wish could be far out of line, such as wishing for a very expensive automobile. When the transit passes and the warranty has expired, the engine breaks down and requires replacement. Then there are insufficient funds to repair it. In the past, the person did have problems of this kind, which is the reason for this placement. If wishes are used wisely and no more than could be easily handled is wished for, there will be sufficient funds to make repairs.

This is a beneficial placement for hopes and wishes, especially for the person who has had a difficult time in achieving hopes and wishes throughout the lifetime. It will be one who has had a particularly difficult and hard life with nothing working out beneficially. This will be a very fortunate time, however it does bring a naive quality to the person so that he or she must be careful and be aware of this erratic placement. Yet, it does bestow a blessing to the individual even though it is for a short period of time.

Advise the person that this is a good time to apply for a raise if he or she had been turned down many times and had given up asking. However, there will definitely be some kind of an increase in income even though it may come from an alternate source.

Jupiter in the Twelfth House

This is an excellent placement. It brings happiness to the person who has been through a very difficult, sorrowful period of time.

This is a benefit in matters of the psychic and one who is employed in a hospital or institution of some kind. It will benefit the native financially. The person will learn to bring spirituality to a much misguided life for it will be a good placement as long as the focus is on spirituality and the artistic benefits of this planet. It is good for developing psychic talents even though the person does not have psychic ability or intuition. The native will begin to have dreams that are true and say such things as, "Gee, I think of things and they happen . . . am I creating this or am I just learning to focus on something?" However, it would be difficult for the person who has a strange or conservative religious background. In this case, it would be beneficial to resolve this background through dreams or intuitive experiences.

The individual who is psychic will find that this ability is coming through greater and better than before. This is the time to expand or develop other skills within their psychic realm. For example, it can be the person who only had the ability of automatic writing, but now has precognitive dreams or has intuition so strong that the minds of others can be read. It greatly expands present knowledge of these gifts. Dreams would be happy, of course.

This placement does not work in a negative manner, and it does not induce a person to take drugs or become an alcoholic. One who had been drinking excessively prior to this placement will benefit by learning to work within a rehabilitation center or institution. This is the time when the native will learn he or she has the will to overcome this problem. This will not bring about destructive actions, but it could if there is a conjunction of Neptune to this planet. The natal placement should be consulted to determine this.

In reviewing the action of this planet through the houses, it can be seen that it helps the individual overcome past difficulties signified by the house placement. In other words, it rectifies something that the individual endured, or was forced to endure, in the past. It is a blessing to the person who experienced the difficulties and continued to live the life that was chosen.

Saturn—The Character Builder

Although this planet brings responsibility, it is the character of the person that determines how that responsibility is handled. Of great importance is to look to the position of this planet in the natal chart. This reveals the area where the individual will be affected. How the person builds character is based upon life experiences and in what area the life revolves.

If the person does not learn the lessons this planet brings, he or she is destined to redo it, for this is not an easy planet. It causes upheaval in some way in the life of everyone, with emotional types having a more difficult time. Stability is the key and a test of character.

Saturn in the First House

The native takes on a great deal of responsibility, which brings about a very dour and somber personality. The added responsibility and the excitement it brings is not recognized for what it truly means. This brings on responsibility for an older person, the less fortunate, or one who is having financial problems. Although the responsibility may be taken graciously, the intensity of this planet eventually wears the person down, and he or she ultimately sheds the responsibility, thus causing a depressed personality. The native feels the weight of the world on his or her shoulders.

If this planet is well-aspected in the natal chart, the native will have the strength of character to work through this difficult configuration, thereby building character. This individual is the contemplative thinker, one who plans ahead and is concerned about the future. Although the native appears to have a dour personality, in reality he or she is much absorbed in thought.

How an individual deals with the situations this planet brings determines the character. If responsibility is shed, it will work to adversely affect the character. In any event, the action of this planet will prevail, especially with respect to those areas of its natal placement. For example, if its natal placement is in the seventh house, the native could choose to wreck a marriage, a contract, a public appearance, or a relationship. But this placement will bring a just reward in the end for the individual will lose all the way around.

Saturn in the Second House
The restrictions of this planet cause a year of difficulty with finances. Resources will be exhausted because of requirements placed upon the native shown by its natal placement. This can be a tricky position, and even a natal fixed star or planetary placement can adversely affect it.

The native will find financial resources burdened, and will have to work hard to make way through the restrictions. The individual could owe the government money or be responsible for someone close who is in financial need. Another side to this tricky position is that it can indicate one who benefits by working for the government or benefits through an inheritance. Either way, it will be difficult because so much effort is placed by earthlings on the physical and material.

The native with the sign Capricorn on the natal Ascendant will find this placement not so difficult and will take it much more graciously. However, eventually it will be determined that it was not such a desirable experience. This is not a favorable time for constructing a house or a building. The individual will find that the original excitement and challenge in its construction will evaporate with the realization that the cost of construction is far more than originally expected. The native will be grateful for the experience and the knowledge learned, but it will have been an expensive lesson.

In building character, it will be one who takes the responsibility in bringing financial aid to the less fortunate. It will be an incarnation where the individual has chosen to work for the less fortunate. The extra responsibility will be shown by its natal position. Even though the natal position is aspected negatively, it does not mean that the person will use it this way. For example, with the natal placement of this planet in the eighth house, and the solar return position in this house, the individual will wish to set up a fund for retirement, purchase insurance, or plan an inheritance to benefit children, grandchildren, or others. It will be the character of the individual shining through.

Saturn in the Third House

This signifies the loss of a relative, or the loss of communication with a relative or relatives. This can also signify the loss of the voice or the ability to communicate in some way. This is not an easy placement. It is a very emotional position for most individuals since it brings about problems with relatives or through the death of a relative. It also indicates a responsibility for a relative or problems with short journeys. It is not be advisable for the native to do much travelling this solar return year. However, it can indicate a journey that is necessary due to the loss of a relative or someone close to the native.

For building character, the person should take responsibility for a relative if the need arises. If the individual has no relatives, or is not involved with relatives in any way, he or she could be active in some area of communications. Look for the character of the person through the natal position to determine the outcome of this placement. For example, one with a natal placement in the fifth house will take on the responsibility of communication with children or siblings. It can be one who develops a method of communication for those who cannot speak or teaches children to communicate.

Saturn in the Fourth House

This is a karmic position. It brings responsibility in the home, such as a member of the family returning home for care. It is the karmic responsibility of the native to care for the person because the one who needs care had taken care of the native in the past. This is not necessarily a mother or father; it could be a parental figure. The native will be repaying a karmic debt through the process of caring for someone by bringing that person into the home or assuming financial responsibility for him or her. It will be a difficult year which will have its effect in the solar return year and beyond.

Negatively, the native could abuse the person brought into the home or simply neglect the person. This will have an adverse effect on the character of the native and bring on a guilt complex. It will reflect a low character or one who does not have a reputable character—a person who is not spiritually stable.

Placing an elderly parent, for example, into a home and then simply neglecting to see that the parent is well taken care of is bad karma. The native must pay back what was given. The outcome can be very beneficial or be greatly detrimental, depending on how the native handles the situation. Either way, it is going to have an emotional effect on the native.

If the person who needs care is advanced in age, this position can be interpreted as death, but it would have to be toward the end of that person's life.

Saturn in the Fifth House
Responsibility for a child, a loved one, or the loss of a loved one or child is indicated with this placement. This could be a loss in the sense of the permanent removal of a child such as would occur in a divorce situation. This can also bring on a lover or a child who is very domineering, one who restricts the native's time, happiness, freedom, and joy. For example, the love interest could be a gambler or one who likes to take chances, and when the luck runs out, the native would be blamed for the losses.

This placement indicates added responsibilities if the native is involved in places of entertainment. Additional grief will be added with the responsibility.

Another side to this position is that the native takes on the responsibility and involvement with anything of a Capricorn nature, such as one who loves a country ruled by Capricorn, a person who is a Capricorn, or a child who is Capricorn in nature. If the native is given this responsibility and handles it appropriately, without abuse, it indicates character building. However, if this position is used negatively, the individual will be of low character and harmful to children in some way. The position and aspects of this planet in the natal chart show how the native handles the responsibility which lasts only through the solar year.

Saturn in the Sixth House

Health is always a problem with this placement and it could involve the skin or bones. There is an adverse effect with employment, such as being hurt on the job. This definitely reflects problems related to the health and also the added responsibility of employment. There will be extra responsibilities on the job thrust upon the native. This also involves pets and the possibility of the loss or an injury to a pet.

The native could take on the responsibility for the health of those in poverty or improve the health of others. This depends upon the placement of this planet in the natal chart. The native will be building character by volunteering to work in the areas of health for the less fortunate or those with a serious disease.

The native can take on more responsibility at work but either does a poor job or improves conditions. This planet is the great teacher and taking on responsibility in a positive manner brings out character. The native can feel the negative effect of this placement at the beginning of the solar return, but as he or she becomes more involved and realizes the system cannot be changed, the native learns to work within it.

Saturn in the Seventh House

The native becomes involved with the legal system in some way, such as a divorce, and becomes obligated for alimony and child support. This is indicative of a breakup of a partnership with added responsibilities. Although it may be assumed by the native that he or she is relieving oneself from the responsibility of a wife and family, this position just brings more responsibility and problems with the system. This does bring problems with a spouse or it can be difficulties because of the loss of a spouse, either in death or in separation.

Marriage can be beneficial if the other person is much older, but in any event the person the native marries restricts him or her in some manner. The greatest impact of the restriction could be determined from the natal position and aspects of this planet.

The placement can indicate one who works as a mediator or helping those involved in divorce. Others will find they have an affinity for unusual art or art connected with ancient ruins. This is a responsible activity for it brings knowledge to the public with respect to a particular civilization. Negatively, it is one who destroys or damages these artifacts, or one who takes responsible action and presents them to the public.

An individual employed within a court system who is responsible for righting social injustices and wrongs done to many people would be character building. It all depends on the power of the personality of the individual, in addition to ability and strength of character.

Saturn in the Eighth House
The placement is not as severe as one may expect. It is one who could benefit through an inheritance, one who accepts responsibility for the affairs of others, the purchase of more insurance for others, or working with the occult in some way. In working with the occult, there will be a temporary separation or a loss of work for some reason. The individual could accept more responsibility in the area of the occult, but either way the outcome of this placement depends on the position of Saturn in the natal chart. There can be a limitation placed on the psychic ability in some way.

The individual who expects to receive money from an insurance company or an inheritance will encounter problems or a delay in receiving the benefits. If the natal chart position of this planet is well aspected, it will be one who benefits from this placement. More than likely, however, there will be responsibility connected to a death, or the necessity of dealing with insurance companies, legacies, a hospice, the occult, and all those matters related to the affairs of this house. In any event, individuals with this position will not want to purchase an insurance policy on themselves.

Sex involves this house, and negatively it will be the individual who decides to become sexually dysfunctional. Working with this position in a positive manner will be the person who is involved with sex therapy or therapy in general, or helping a person overcome sexual difficulties. One who has learned life's lessons will be responsible and grow from the experience. Later in life, the individual will take on a spiritual nature which will be reflected in the character.

Saturn in the Ninth House

Difficulties will arise with a professional person, or the native is restrained from acquiring a higher education or journey that was planned. This can also be one who takes on the responsibility of another in the course of travel. This is the parent who is backing a child financially to become educated in some profession. It is also the individual who finds it difficult to find the financing for a graduate course at college.

The native will find his\her philosophy of life greatly tested which can bring on an emotional time; but this planet is in the house of Jupiter so its effect is eased. The native will take the positive spiritual side of Saturn only in later years, and will look to an older individual to find spirituality. This is difficult for philosophy and the native will find this an area difficult to easily accept. It would, therefore, be avoided. Based on the character, an older person with this placement will benefit greatly.

The solar return must be based on that which the individual has chosen to do in this lifetime. Someone who has nothing to do with foreign journeys will probably not feel any effects in this area. However, someone in a teaching capacity will wish to study the philosophies of the ancients and then pass the information on to students and others. It also indicates the person who desires to go back to school to earn a degree in some profession.

Saturn in the Tenth House
The native finds other areas of responsibility involving career. There will be difficulties with the government or one working with the government in an area relating to the native's career. The individual will experience difficulties with the career or accept additional responsibility with the career. Either way, it will be restrictive and difficult. Another side to this placement is the individual who is working towards a promotion in the chosen career. In addition, this is not a good position for the person who is entering politics, nor would it be a good time to accept employment or seek assistance from a government agency.

Although not directly affected by it, the native may hear of a parent going through a difficult period. There will be no burden placed upon the native, but he or she may be called upon to help in some way.

This is a placement of character building if the native does his or her best to overcome the difficulties encountered. The natal placement of this planet is important. For example, the third house signifies one who chooses to communicate facts surrounding certain heritages, cultures, or government subsidies, or one who exposes government or corporate corruption. If the person exposes government or corporate waste and corruption for selfish gains, it reflects a spiritually unbalanced person. But a whistleblower who takes on this responsibility without anticipating rewards will build character, especially when a job is lost as a result or other unfortunate things happen. A whistleblower could even be a child telling on a sibling who is doing something against the wishes of the parents.

Saturn in the Eleventh House

A limitation or loss of income can be the result of this placement, as well as a limitation on the native's hopes and wishes. It brings older friendships and a responsibility of some kind in an organization. This is not a difficult position and it will be short in duration. It would not be advisable to join an organization for the first time during this transit.

The person can become interested in some field of study during the transit, but as the year moves on, a change is made to another field. A person building character is one who can handle the responsibility of the erratic effect of this placement. This planet does not have a strong influence in this house. Hopes and wishes and income are brought about with this placement if the person takes the time to determine what he or she truly wishes to have. For example, it would be a good time to invest or join an organization that would provide an income during the later years of life. Building character is determined by the way the native deals with friends, or one who takes responsibility for a friend who is in poverty.

Saturn in the Twelfth House

This is truly the position of character building. This affects the individual through sorrows, spending time in a hospital, or spending more time challenging groups who spread certain misguided philosophies and ideologies. The native will discover that these groups are secret enemies. This is not a good time to enter the hospital as there is a probability of catching a disease; nor is it a good time to be involved with mental or large institutions of any type, including religious institutions. Although this is not the time to work with the occult, it is a good time for the individual to realize that the occult is truly a benefit, contrary to what has been said by certain individuals or groups.

This is the house of confinement; thus the native will be imprisoned if he or she elects to do something illegal. With this placement, the native will certainly be caught and imprisoned. Individuals who have been leading responsible lives and have taken the high road will avoid this kind of life. Either way, the native will be involved either through association or by becoming directly implicated. This position definitely results in the person being restricted in some way, even though it may be for a short period of time. This is a placement that can lead to a higher or lower road, depending on what the person seeks in life.

With respect to illegal drugs or alcohol, this is not a position where one is induced to become an addict or alcoholic. It is the former alcoholic or drug addict who has taken responsibility for helping others overcome their addictions.

At some point, this transit will be detrimental to the individual. How he or she chooses to overcome the difficulty will determine the building of character. The native may either become bitter, and thus lose through bitterness, or learn from the lessons this planet brings. Consult its natal placement to determine strength of character. One who is very sensitive with many water signs in weak positions will probably not be able to overcome such a difficult placement.

Uranus—Unique Creativity

This is the planet of genius, but it can be quite adverse in its actions. It is truly an erratic planet, and it would be best if individuals were to apply it in a positive manner; that is, creatively unique. It takes a genius to create from a mental standpoint for all creativity comes from the mental or from the spiritual plane. Thus the individual would be applying the creative forces of the universe. It is plugging into the electrical force that is the source of creativity. Brilliant thought patterns and ideas come in rapidly but will leave just as quickly, so action must be taken immediately on these creatively unique ideas.

Uranus in the First House
This gives the native an unusual year and a very unusual outlook throughout the period. There are flashes of wisdom that come

and go. The mind is unable to hold on to an idea for more than a few seconds. The individual should carry a notebook at all times to write down concepts because it will be a difficult time to remember what was achieved during the year. This is a position where the native feels the surge of energy, ideas, and thought patterns to the point where there is difficulty sleeping. The native feels extremely energized. They tendency will be to burn oneself out through an attempt to continuously tap into this energy continuously, thus causing periods of anxiety.

Uranus in the Second House

The individual will develop unique ideas surrounding matters dealing with money and personal possessions. This is the time for the individual to develop a unique concept in earning money. If the individual is in the field of banking, he or she should apply these uniquely creative ideas to the banking system or other institutions involved with money, stocks, bonds, and other financial matters.

Great thoughts and ideas will be for a short period of time, and if not acted upon, will not materialize. Action must be taken on these unique concepts within this planet's solar year, as this placement will not occur again.

Uranus in the Third House

This is brilliance involving communication and any form of writing. This could be a year that a great psychic ability comes to them. The person should write down all that is being received. He or she will be able to write funny humor or uniquely entertaining humor. It will be any type of creativity expressed in the form of writing or in communications. Another side to this is the person who makes fun of a relative. The native should be advised that there will be difficulty in closing down the mind and thus the point of exhaustion could be reached.

Although not generally important with respect to short travels, this could be the person who develops a unique or brilliant idea with respect to trips connected with sports or some other activity.

Natives must write down and apply their brilliant ideas during the cycle. Most individuals with this placement will not apply their uniquely created ideas.

Uranus in the Fourth House

The native would bring about unique features in the home. This is a good placement for a building contractor who brings in uniquely creative concepts in construction. Even though the native is not connected with the building industry, he or she will have brilliant ideas in this area—although they will not be applied in a productive way. There will be uniquely creative ideas formed with respect to all areas of this house that the native did not have prior to this placement. However, it will be only for the brief solar period and must be acted upon during this time.

The individual will contemplate changing the residence, but will not necessarily make the changes unless the are acted upon it within the solar return year. The native will think about it, but not act upon the idea. He or she will, however, bring new ideas into the home through different ways of cooking meals or decorating, for example.

Uranus in the Fifth House

There will be unusual concepts in helping children to learn or for the entertainment of children. This will also be the person who will have an unusual lover during this solar year or one who will be involved in an unusual adventure. It will only be enjoyed for a short period of time, however, since a person would not wish to be involved with children every day for the rest of his or her life, nor be involved with unusual adventures continuously.

The individual can bring new ideas into sports if they are acted upon within this cycle. The pattern of the person's life is important here. For example, if the native is a homemaker, some of these interpretations would not apply. However, even though the individual is a homemaker, he or she could develop unique ideas involving areas pertaining to children, such as creating unique ideas with respect to after school activities for sports and the entertainment of children.

This is a very good position for the reason that it brings the native much happiness and pleasure through all matters pertaining to this house. The effect of this placement will be brief unless this planet is in the same house in the natal chart.

Uranus in the Sixth House

This is a good position for the native to bring new concepts into the workforce. Others would consider the unique ideas strange, but once the individual explains the brilliance behind the concepts, it could bring a promotion or increase in pay. The native could also be the one who comes up with various ideas pertaining to work and health but does nothing about it. Individuals simply do not realize that their ideas are brilliant.

With respect to health, the person could come up with concepts related to health and to those employed in the health field, but again, unless this position is well aspected, the person will have a fleeting idea but not act upon that idea.

Uranus in the Seventh House

More than any other time in life, the native will be speaking or appearing before the public. An individual working as a marriage counselor could develop unique ideas for those who wish to get married. This also can be the person who decides to get married in a unique way, such as being married while sky diving or bungy jumping, which could bring publicity as well. It would be very creative but also difficult to get others to go along with the unique idea.

The native is well qualified to speak before the public for there would be an electrifying quality to the delivery. Although one may not be involved in the public arena, the native will still create unique ideas, but they will not accomplish anything with respect to the public or public matters.

This is a rapid fire position when involved with the judicial system. One who has a negative natal position for marriage but decides that this is the year to get married will find that it will have an unfavorable outcome. Initially, the native will think the marriage is electrifying and exciting, but they will find that the great excitement was only for the duration of the transit.

This will benefit one who is an attorney or a politician. These people will bring about brilliant ideas to benefit the public. It will be a very good time for them to tour the country giving public lectures. They will be in demand throughout the solar year.

Uranus in the Eighth House
There will be unusual sex or unusual developments for the native who works in the field of insurance or is involved with insurance in some way. This is also the one who suddenly receives psychic flashes, especially from deceased loved ones. This will be exciting or frightening, depending on the person's upbringing. The flashes and visions will come quickly and leave quickly. The person will be uncertain of what has been seen because of the fleeting incident. There are periods when there will be psychic flashes that affect the native's life.

With respect to death, it does indicate the person will have a flash concerning a death that will not necessarily be adverse or involve the native. The person could hear of a death or have a premonition pertaining to the death of someone, but it will be more of psychic flash than anything else. The individual will develop brilliant concepts applying to the matters of this house during this solar period, but they must be acted upon during this period.

Uranus in the Ninth House
This is a good position for developing the spiritual side of life. The native will wish to learn as much as possible during this period. The native can make great advances in his/her own spirituality because of positive psychic flashes. There will be good and positive experiences that will be uplifting to the individual. This is

also a good time for the native to pass on philosophy to others. The individual will have insight into concepts he or she never understood before, such as the ability to define certain parts of the Bible or the philosophy that is related to the Bible or other religions. This is a great period for elevating oneself spiritually.

There will be concepts with respect to journeys, and whether the journeys will be only mental or physical will depend on the lifestyle of the person. The individual could travel and lecture on various topics of philosophy, religion, or astrology, which will bring knowledge to others. This will depend on the soul development of the individual. This also can be one who brings unique and brilliant concepts to the professional and legal departments of a university.

Uranus in the Tenth House

The native will be considering a unique career change. This will be a move because of a concept that brought the native recognition. It could also be a move because of a promotion brought about by brilliant ideas, such as developing a new computerized system that greatly helped the corporation or government. The individual may or may not put these ideas to use. If the individual is not involved with a corporation or the government, this placement can be used to work on the career or career changes. Although it could bring about the conception that the native should make a career change, it would not necessarily be a good time to make the change. The native could come up with a brilliant idea that brings a promotion, but after the solar year ends he or she cannot handle the new job. It depends on the individual and the transits of the other planets affecting this placement.

Uranus in the Eleventh House

The person brings great concepts to an organization or to income from the career or involvements with friends, but it could all backfire on the individual. The ideas and concepts may seem good at the time but they will more than likely cause problems later. It is not a good position for changing organizations. The native will join an organization, decide to take it over, and become involved and excited with it, but then becomes upset and moves away, leaving the damage behind.

The individual could develop a brilliant idea to make more money, but it would end up costing more than is made. This is a placement where the individual should be advised not to make changes involving this house placement during the solar year because the changes will more than likely cause problems at a later date. Neither is this a time for hopes and wishes or new friendships.

Uranus in the Twelfth House

This is a karmic position. It is a good placement for intuitive and psychic development. There will be unusual dreams with flashes of brilliance relating to the dreams, dream interpretations, or any type of psychological activity. The person could bring about brilliant concepts through the dream state, but may not remember them upon awakening.

The native will bring benefits to an institution through unique concepts and ideas relating to employment. It brings the person insight for the period of the solar year. The person must choose to be more spiritual to avoid the adverse affects of this placement. For example, it could be one who develops a new drug or medication and then has it backfire later or one who enters a hospital due to an erratic mental behavior.

This is a very tricky position, and the individual should be advised that it will be far better to receive brilliant ideas through dreams and intuition and not depend on drugs or other alternative sources to help develop new concepts. This placement should be very well aspected before the individual develops new concepts and ideas because the so-called brilliant ideas could place the native in an institution or a prison. With this placement the native should stay within the spiritual realm and not try to find spirituality through drugs in order to alter and highlight spirituality.

Neptune—The Great Illusion

This is the planet of dreamlike thought patterns that are inspirational and illusionary. It is illusion connected to that which is inspirational. Inspiration and illusion go hand in hand in every placement of the chart. Dreams can be fantasies as well as inspirations, but they should not be acted upon during the solar year. When Neptune is used in a positive manner, it is spiritual and inspirational. When it is used negatively, it becomes deception and disillusionment.

Neptune in the First House

The individual will have the look of one who is in a dreamlike state, vacillating between reality and the dream state. The native can easily be inspired by the beautiful and the creative, such as music and the arts but can also be easily distracted. The native is often so lost in the dream state that he or she is unable to act upon inspirations. Natives receive psychic flashes that they truly believe will give them the ability to accomplish a great deal. But more often than not, they never really achieve or act upon their inspirations.

This is an opportune time for these individuals to become involved in studies that allow their creativity to flow. They receive psychic flashes that they believe will give them the ability to accomplish anything they wish. They can discover an art form, such as music, and then spend most of their time listening to music without being productive or applying themselves directly to that art form.

During the solar year the native will not believe he or she is being deceptive or under an illusion. This is the position of self-deception and thus very little would be accomplished with respect to the matters of the sign and house placement.

Neptune in the Second House

The native should not become involved with financial affairs, as resources could be lost if the native is inspired to invest or make expensive purchases. There is inspiration to earn more money through creative endeavors, but this is a time when the native could lose financially. Individuals who have this planet predominant in the natal chart will be affected more by this transit than anyone else. They will be more apt to get into certain types of financial endeavors they feel are worthy, but in reality they will be under an illusion and deception.

This is not a fortunate time to spend money or invest. If the individual is inspired to be involved in some type of financial or business investment for example, he or she should record the inspirations but delay the transaction until after the solar year. It will then be seen as a truly inspirational idea or as deception and not worthy of consideration.

Neptune in the Third House

This placement indicates a person who will be inspired by creative endeavors with respect to writing or in the communications field. The native will also be involved with deceptive relatives, neighbors, or siblings. The individual should be advised not to spend any money on a relative, as the end result will be unfortunate. It is important to note that with this planet the person is inspired with those things of this house. It is truly a gift, but the inspiration should not be acted upon until after the solar year. Individuals who have this placement can develop creative writing skills or have relatives with creative writing skills, but it would be best to put the skills in motion after the end of the transit.

This is also an opportune time for the native to think about taking short journeys. The ideas born of this transit should be recorded but not put into motion until after the end of the transit.

Neptune in the Fourth House

Individuals are under an illusion with respect to the home, and it is an emotional year for them. They do believe they know what is best and they are truly inspired by their emotional feelings, but they need to be very cautious in what they do. This is not the time to bring another into the home, as the person brought into the home will turn out to be highly detrimental to the native. This person will cause problems and deception for the length of time he or she remains in the home, and this could be for many years.

The individual may be inspired to decorate the home, but it would not be wise to begin such a project until the following solar year. The ideas will be brilliant and they will be good for the home, but action must wait until after the transit.

This is the time the person becomes involved with the psychic realm, but communication with spirit entities should not take place in the home at this time. The possibility of contact with negative spirit entities would be much greater, and information received from spirits can be deceptive, confused, or not in the best interests of the native.

Neptune in the Fifth House

It is the year of falling in love, either with a lover, admiration for a child, or entertainment. The native should not act upon any inspiring idea for creating entertainment or amusements for others as he or she will certainly lose financially during this transit. It is a good time to bring forth new concepts and ideas with respect to entertainment or a lover, but it is not the time to follow through with inspiring thoughts.

The native can be inspired by a lover, and it can be a very inspiring relationship, but inspiration and illusion work together so that the native will be easily deceived by the relationship. The native will not listen to anyone who issues warnings, since he or she truly believes the one he or she is in love with is the perfect match.

It is not the year for investing, speculation, and sports. It is a good time to bring forth inspiring ideas involving these areas, but they should not be acted upon until the conclusion of the transit.

Neptune in the Sixth House

Health problems are indicated with this placement, and the native will be under an illusion as to the diagnosis of his/her own ailment, believing he/she has a keen insight into it and passing this information on to others. To use this placement correctly, the native must record inspirations but not follow through with them because it will be dangerous to diagnose their health problem and the health problems of others at this time. If the person has a strong background in the health field and the aspects to this planet are strong and beneficial, this will not be damaging; but if the native has no background in the health care field, much damage can result.

With respect to the workplace, the native will become the know-it-all at work, with great ideas to improve the working environment. However, the individual will not see the ideas as a detriment. This is a period of deception in the workplace, and it indicates deception either by the native or the deceptive practices of others.

This is not an appropriate year to adopt a pet, but it is certainly a good time to help an organization such as the humane society. Helping such an organization would be of great inspiration to the native, but not if one personally becomes involved with an animal. There will also be the possibility of contracting a disease through a pet. The individual will be inspired to help animals at this time, but this should be done only through organizations, not as a personal endeavor.

Neptune in the Seventh House
The public becomes the inspiration and the native will feel that concepts and inspirational ideas should be brought before the public or, depending on the nature of the ideas, try to make them legal. It is not wise to follow through with the ideas at this time.

This is an inspiration for marriage, but not the time to get married, nor to force their ideas on the partner. The native will develop concepts surrounding the creative forces of marriage, such as new ideas to make marriage more beautiful, but these concepts should not be enacted for they could turn out to be destructive. Inspirations with matters of this house bring on overconfidence, deception, and illusion. This position indicates a person who is inspired by marriage, the public, the courts, lawyers, and all other areas of this house, but the native can at the same time be deceived. The inspirational concepts can be excellent; it is just that they cannot be carried out during the solar return year.

It is advisable for the individual to avoid litigation. One should not go into court unless it is with someone totally trustworthy. With this configuration, even the attorney chosen to represent the native will be his/her undoing.

Neptune in the Eighth House

This is an excellent placement for developing psychic gifts. The individual will be more cautious in developing the psychic ability because of the secret nature of this house. It is be one who will be more fearful and therefore not rush into any particular psychic concept. This is the time to work with others in developing the psychic ability, but it is not a good time to attempt it on one's own. This is the best position for this planet because the individual becomes more cautious in what is done with respect to the matters of this house, thus allowing it to work to the benefit of the individual.

The person should be advised not to become involved with insurance matters of any kind. If at all possible, one should not purchase any type of insurance at this time. Renewing an existing policy will not create a problem, but purchasing a new policy will turn out to be detrimental in some way.

This is an indication of the death of someone known to the native, but it can also be a contact with one known to the person who is in spirit.

There are other matters of this house that will be affected by this position; however, the most important interpretation for this powerful placement is psychic development. This is the time the native becomes aware of other universal forces and becomes less fearful of spiritual forces and the unknown.

Neptune in the Ninth House

Great and inspiring ideas are developed at this time—ideas of a philosophical nature and concepts beneficial for many people. But the inspirational concepts and philosophy can become lost unless the native has a strong, levelheaded background that can inspire others in philosophy of a higher power. If the individual is not a spiritually strong person, there will be involvement instead in frivolous affairs.

In any event, the individual is inspired by philosophy, religion, travel, and higher education. The inspirations should be recorded and brought forth the following year. The inspirations of this planet are brilliant and given to individuals by divine sources. The character of the person will determine the outcome of the ideas and the way the inspirations will be utilized.

The native will be inspired to return to school and to continue education, but it is not a good time to actually put it into effect. It is only the time to research courses, determine costs, and decide the school or college to attend.

Neptune in the Tenth House

The individual should be advised not to become involved with the government in any way. This includes divulging illegal matters to government authorities or criticizing the competency of others in government. It is not the time for the individual to admit anything about self to any government agency.

It is a time when the native becomes inspired to make a career change or becomes inspired with ideas and concepts related to the career; however, one should not act on it at this time because the changes would not be seen clearly. This planet inspires, but also confuses, so that action on concepts brought through inspirational thoughts should be delayed until the transit has passed.

Neptune in the Eleventh House

This is a good placement for the individual who wishes to be involved with an organization or to join a certain organization; however, it is not a favorable placement for a long lasting commitment to an organization. The native will be inspired to be involved with a certain group for financial gain or to learn from it, but the person should not expect anything from the association with the group until the following solar return. This is a good time to learn from a group, and for those who are loners, it would be a favorable period to participate in organizations. this is a good transit for involving oneself in those groups whose activities and goals would normally have been ignored.

This is one who can be inspired by a friend, but it will not be a favorable period to act upon the advice of friends. It will be a favorable time for the native to make new friends who have the same interests; however, the friendships should not be too close during this transit for there is the possibility of manipulation and deception through these newly formed friendships.

Neptune in the Twelfth House

The duality of this planet is much in evidence with this placement. This is the individual who becomes greatly inspired to help the less fortunate or to help those confined in prisons or institutions, but at the same time, the native is easily deceived by his/her own inspiring thoughts. One should act on the inspirations after the transit has passed.

It is a favorable period to study those matters of a psychic nature or the dream world, including dream interpretations, as the person can develop much higher skills with this subject than ever expected. Learn the concepts and record the information to be applied when the solar year has ended.

This is the year for the native to decide to take the high road and not the low road in life. It is not the time to take drugs or alcohol to develop psychic gifts for one will find at a later time that what was received was neither inspiring nor truly helpful. The individual must use caution when involved with this placement. It is not the time to apply any spirit messages that have been received, or any inspiring concepts, without others being present who are experienced and who have a strong background in this area.

Entering a hospital for observation or diagnosis is favorable. However, this is not the time to enter a hospital for surgery or to cure an illness. If at all possible, it is best to enter the hospital at the end of the solar year. The danger of contracting infection while in the hospital is much greater with this transit. It is the time when the individual may become addicted to a medication prescribed during a hospital visit. Taking drugs and medication for an illness must be kept to a minimum. The person should not trust the intuition as to the length of time a drug or medication is necessary.

Involvement with a secret enemy is very possible during this solar return year. The native can become involved with a secret enemy and not realize it. The individual should use great care in taking advice from others, unless it is a certainty that the advice is being given by one the native knows well and who has been trusted for a long period of time.

Pluto—The Great Power

Pluto has a powerful effect on the solar return chart of the individual. Although it is taught that this planet affects the masses, it also affects the individual personally and the relationship with the masses. It is a power position for that particular year, but its effect can last beyond the solar return. The aspects affecting the placement are important in that they will determine how the power will be used. Unfortunate aspects of planets to this position of power can be quite devastating. Pluto is a dual planet for its power can be used to benefit others or it can be used destructively. It is not considered a spiritual planet, but instead it can be called the planet of psychic power.

Pluto in the First House

The native experiences a great psychic surge and a power never realized in life. This is a position where the old belief system is torn down and a new belief system adopted. The native will wish to become more involved with this surge of dramatic psychic energy, and can use it selfishly to abuse others or learn to deal with it in a manner that would be beneficial to self and others.

The character of the individual is very important when determining the outcome of this powerful transit, because it's possible to be very domineering and dictatorial to the point of cruelty. On a higher level, one will use this gift for the betterment of others. Either way, the person will feel this power and will use it as the character dictates.

This is the planet of death and at this time the native will develop an understanding of death related matters, such as the individual who can predict a death or one who helps the police investigate a murder. It does not indicate the death of the native. Choosing to use this power in a negative way, however, can cause the individual to have a fatal accident or be killed in an underworld shooting.

Pluto in the Second House
This placement indicates a most fortunate time to invest for the native will have the power and ability to attract material possessions or to realize a monetary or physical gain. This is the year the native will have the ability to attract wealth. Depending on aspects to this planet, it can tear down one's former earning ability and instead bring about a new source of income. The native will have a psychic gift involving financial affairs and material possessions in addition to all other affairs of this house. The person must be careful not to become tyrannical about possessions.

Using this position for criminal activity will allow the individual to get away with it for a short time, but ultimately one will pay the consequences unless aspects continue to be favorable, but this would be rare. Using the psychic power against the masses will eventually bring about severe penalties to the individual and everything will be lost.

Pluto in the Third House

The individual suddenly finds a great ability to communicate well, including communication with relatives. There are good ideas about teaching, travel, and communications. The person will be drawn to work in these areas for he or she has developed a strong feeling toward this side of their life. Although one may not ever choose to work in the matters of this house, there will be an ability for this type of career.

There is the possibility of the death of a relative while on a trip. It does not always occur, but the indication is present with this configuration. This, of course, will cause a great deal of communication between relatives and others.

The individual will do well with the written word, writing psychic books and lecturing on psychic awareness, especially if the person has a metaphysical background.

Pluto in the Fourth House

There is power in the home with this placement, more so than at any other time. The native will bring new concepts and abilities to the home and family, taking a leadership role with respect to the home and family. It is a strong placement for dealing with emotions. There will be a transformation involving the home and family.

Death can never be shown in the chart of an individual. However, this is a position that can indicate the death of a dominant parent. It can also indicate the death of a home or another matter of this house. A poor aspect to this placement can bring about an accident in the home, cause a death in the home, or it can simply change the power structure in the home.

The influence of the native over the dominant parent is very possible with this placement. It will be a time when the dominant parent is looking to the native for a leadership role within the family structure.

Pluto in the Fifth House

This indicates a powerful love affair, a love for a child, or a love affair with sports and entertainment, which would include gambling and speculation. There is a strong feeling within to take up the idea of gaming or gambling in some way. This will depend on aspects. In any case, it is a favorable position for the most part.

Although this does not necessarily indicate the death of a child, it can be the transformation or removal of the child from the control of the native. This is also the person who has the ability to control and direct a very disruptive child during this transit.

This is a good placement for the person who has a low sex drive. Because of an intense love affair, stamina for sex would be recouped. There can also be the loss of a lover because obsession drives the person away. This depends on aspects to this placement, such as an opposition or square of Mars and Saturn. A conjunction of Uranus would bring a change in a relationship, a strange love affair, or one who is attracted to the unusual or the unique.

Pluto in the Sixth House

This is an excellent position for a person who has had poor health. This placement will bring about the restoration of the health of the individual. It helps the native strengthen self to overcome health problems. The native had unusually poor aspects to this house in a former life and is now given this placement to benefit the healing process.

There is power in employment and through others in the workforce, and a strong influence over coworkers. The power can be used to help organize coworkers for a certain cause. It is an indicator of one who will have great leadership abilities in the workplace.

The native will have the ability at this time to deal with pets, or if there are negative aspects to this placement, it indicates a person who could be cruel to pets and animals. This depends on the overall character of the individual.

Pluto in the Seventh House

The native will have the ability to appear before the public and engage in many speaking engagements through the courtroom, news media, or radio and television. The ability will exist to strengthen a labor union, for example, if involved in this type of organization

This placement does not necessarily bring about a union of marriage, but simply a union of partnership, or it helps bring about awareness with respect to certain public interests. It brings power to the individual to appear before the public or be involved in a partnership of some kind.

It brings strength to the individual with respect to lawsuits, but the outcome of the litigation will strictly depend upon aspects. This would not be a good time to be involved in litigation if any malefic planets are in opposition.

Pluto in the Eighth House

A strong love for the occult or a great sexual union with another is indicated with this position. The native could have such a strong sex drive during this solar year that he or she would become addicted to sex. There will be sex and psychic experiences at the same time, with the native developing a deep feeling within that he or she is having a psychic experience while engaging in a strong sexual union with another.

It brings power to the affairs of the person involving insurance and money belonging to others. This is a good time for some of the investments that were made previously to return home, especially if the individual invested at a time when this planet was in the second house. It does very often bring about a legacy through the death of another, and it generally works this way; however, it lasts only for the solar return year.

Pluto in the Ninth House

This is an excellent position. The individual has the ability to be charismatic and philosophical, and is able to pass his or her philosophy and beliefs to others. The person would be totally obsessed with philosophy, religion, foreign travel, politics, and all other matters of this house during the solar year. An attorney who has this placement should run for a judgeship or political office. Even those who are corrupt or cruel can achieve power with this placement, but it will turn against them later.

Pluto in the Tenth House
This is an extremely strong placement. It indicates the person who is very effective in career matters and desires to oversee other people. It can be someone who desires to take over the government, a government department or agency, or matters concerning poverty and the government. The individual can take on dictatorial tendencies, but can also bring many benefits to others. The character and nature of the individual would depend on how the power is used. One with compassion will truly wish to help the poor and unfortunate. On the other hand, one with a low character will use it in a cruel and dictatorial way.

If the placement is well aspected, it will be an appropriate time to change jobs or career; that is, if one feels the power has been achieved to move up to a much better and influential position. This position does not necessarily mean that the person will change jobs. The change will likely occur strictly for the power it will bring.

Pluto in the Eleventh House
This is a good position for bringing powerful friends and the ability to communicate to others. It will bring additional income and many of the native's hopes and wishes. For those who were afraid to ask for a raise in salary, this is the time for them to do so since they will have the strength of will to bring it about.

At this time, the individual will have the ability to reorganize a group or organization, or to revitalize one that was torn apart. It can bring about the end of an old relationship or friendship. This is the year for the person to increase the earning potential. It must be emphasized, however, that this placement must be used for the benefit of others; it is the time that the native begins to feel altruistic and can bring benefits to others through unselfishness and compassion.

Pluto in the Twelfth House
The character of the individual and how the life was led, together with the aspects, will determine how the power will be used.

This brings a person with underworld power, a powerful enemy, a devious type in the field of underworld activities, or one involved with all other negative aspects of this planet. On the other hand, it will be one who is inclined to bring about changes for the benefit of others. The native will help those who are unfortunate or mentally ill, or bring about the native's own change from leading life in the underworld to a higher level of existence. This is a position that is potentially very bad or extremely good.

Through dreams or through a dreamlike state, the native may see a loved one who is in spirit or the individual may hear psychic voices. It will more than likely occur during the dream period. This is the time for the person to learn to interpret the dreams of others, or if psychic, to help police uncover facts on the death of a person or to locate one who is missing.

Lilith—The Deceptor

It is an asteroid that brings about minor irritants in the life of individuals, and it can deceive them in such a way that they are not aware of its presence. Its property in the solar return chart is deception, irritation, and frustration, but these incidents are not necessarily intentional. It acts in a less dramatic way than Neptune or the inconjunct aspect. Therefore, it may be identified as Neptune's little brother the gremlin that upsets Earth beings in some way.

Lilith in the First House
The native will be deceived in many ways, and in turn, the person will deceive self with this placement. The deception could be

little white lies, but would be minor irritants just the same. The native should be aware of this during the transit. Even though the native is normally a very conscientious and forthright individual, he or she will find it necessary to tell a white lie for some reason; for example, as an attempt to protect or help another. Others will do the same to the native.

Lilith in the Second House

There will be discrepancies with respect to financial affairs and personal possessions. More care should be taken by the native at this time to avoid problems and mistakes involving banking institutions or other organizations handling money and personal possessions. There will be small deceptions and irritations, but they can lead to major problems later on. The person will be somewhat self-deceptive about the financial condition at this time, so it would be wise to be on the alert for mistakes with respect to financial affairs. The person may not realize how much money has been spent, even though it may be in small increments, and thus be in financial difficulty.

Lilith in the Third House

Deceptive communication and relatives are brought about by this placement. There will be deceptions through the media and other forms of communication. There will be minor irritations and frustrations on short journeys or through relatives. The person should be made aware when writing, whether it is a simple letter or a manuscript, to proofread what has been written. The mistakes will not necessarily be major, but they will be an irritant.

Lilith in the Fourth House

Things around the house become misplaced, lost, or confused, or the native is denied something with respect to affairs of the home and real estate. There will be emotional situations occurring in the home as well, such as irritations involving the dominant parent. The native will find that the parent will tend to be more confused, misplacing objects around the home. The individual will also misplace objects that can involve home and automobile, for example, which can be irritating and frustrating. The native can rest assured that after this transit passes, the lost items will be found and returned.

This would not be an appropriate time to buy furniture or other items for the home as there would be flaws of some kind with the purchase. It would be an irritant, but the individual could live with it. However, this is the time when the individual will buy second-hand objects such as those found at flea markets or used furniture stores.

Lilith in the Fifth House

Individuals will find themselves involved with a truly irritating little person. This will be a child who is constantly getting on one's nerves, or the native will be irritating to a loved one or some other person. This is not an appropriate time to bet at the horse or dog track or play numbers. The choice is always close to being a winner, but the native will always lose, causing irritation and frustration. Irritations will extend to loved ones and all matters of this house placement.

This position brings an irritating child to the native. It will be an especially difficult position for a teacher of young children.

Lilith in the Sixth House

Deceptions in work and health are indicated. This is not the time to accept a diagnosis from just one physician. The person should be advised to get more than one opinion. The native will be irritated with the initial diagnosis, and therefore should get other opinions.

There will be one individual in the workplace who will deceive the native, causing irritations and deceptions. This can involve harmless jokes, for example, that turn out to be falsehoods that bring forth irritations.

Insects will be a problem even to those individuals who are not prone to insect problems. The native will be plagued by mosquitoes, roaches, or other insects. It is an irritant that must be accepted. This is also the person who is deceived into believing there is no infestation, but in truth it is present. The infestation is an irritant, but would not be a major problem.

Lilith in the Seventh House

There will be minor irritations and deceptions involving a partnership, the public, or any type of legal affairs with respect to the public or public matters. The native will find that innocent mistakes are made when invited to address a group or the public—the wrong place or time to appear or a change made in the subject matter. Although the person will find it irritating, it will be something that can be accomplished without difficulty.

Partnerships become a source of irritation and deception, either by the native, the other partner, or both. Mistakes and unintentional deceptions occur. This will not present a problem to most people, but for those with fixed sign placements, it can become quite difficult.

Lilith in the Eighth House

Mistakes and irritations are brought about through all matters of this house. Problems with insurance companies and with the occult are indicated with this placement. If the native is involved with psychics, there will be irritations as a result of emotions the psychics display. Psychics for the most part cannot be depended upon to do what they promise because they are moved by emotions and what may be occurring at the time. Although not intentional, this will cause the native to experience minor irritations and frustrations.

Irritations and frustrations with insurance companies, banking institutions, and other organizations of this type will always occur with this placement. It will not only extend to matters of this house, but to second house matters. It would be wise for the native to closely monitor financial connections with any person or organization.

Lilith in the Ninth House

Irritation with professional individuals or groups is indicated. The native will realize that religious speakers are spreading falsehoods.

Frustrations and innocent mistakes will occur if the individual is attending a university or school. For example, the native could be given the wrong schedule, a computer error or breakdown could occur, or other problems and mistakes could arise causing irritations and frustrations for the individual.

The native can become quite frustrated with his or her philosophy of life. This is the time he or she attempts to discover the falsehoods in beliefs previously held to be true. There will be irritations over religious beliefs, with the native suddenly becoming irritated and frustrated over what he or she has been taught. The native will believe them to be deceptions, which they truly are, but what was adopted in the past as truth will be discovered to be mistaken ideologies.

Lilith in the Tenth House

The individual will be irritated with all matters concerning poverty, welfare, the government, and government or company policies in general. This can cause some harm to the native if he or she becomes too vocal with respect to what is found to be unjust. Those who are having this transit who work for any agency of government or a company should be advised to refrain from verbal and outspoken references to what they deem to be mistakes and deceptions by those in authority.

This is one position where the individual could bring harm to self by being too vocal or disgruntled with career. This is the time one could make an innocent error on a tax return, causing irritations with the additional costs incurred.

Lilith in the Eleventh House

This is irritation with friends caught telling small white lies, but then again, the native returns the procedure. The native will be irritated with just about everything in life, believing he/she has been deceived, especially with hopes and wishes. This is the time the native will feel hopes and wishes have been denied. It is a discouraging time in life for the person believes that hopes and dreams will never be realized. This is brought about by the native's own thoughts and not by an outer influence. Frustrations over the failure to achieve hopes and wishes brings an irritant. It is a minor irritant, but the native does see it as a great disappointment. Although the native tries hard to achieve a higher position with a larger salary, he or she truly believes at this time it will never happen. In any event, it is not an appropriate time to ask for an increase in salary.

The native can deceive a friend or organization at this time or a friend may deceive the individual. This can be brought about by the person feeling he or she is doing something charitable, while really causing more harm than good.

Lilith in the Twelfth House
There will be problems and irritations surrounding institutions. The individual will be frustrated over the mentality and mental outlook. There will be self-deception or deception through others, and frustrations with all matters pertaining to this house placement. The self-deception can be through the dreamlike state or a misinterpretation of a dream. One may have to deal with institutions with which there normally is no contact. This can be the salesperson who dislikes dealing with hospitals but must do so to keep a job.

The native should be advised not to be involved with any matters of this house while this transit is in effect. This is a position that always works negatively. It brings about mistakes, even though they may be unintentional, but a mistake in a hospital can be devastating. A hospital patient with this placement will incur many problems and frustrations, even to the point of being irritated over the person who shares a hospital room. Everything connected with the hospital—nurse, doctor, and others—will be irritating and frustrating to the native.

Part of Fortune

It is a lesser energy than Jupiter, so it can be referred to as Jupiter's little sister. It helps counterbalance negative effects in an area of the chart where it is needed. It is this fortunate point that gives the individual a way out of some problem that arises in the life, but always in a small way.

Part of Fortune in the First House

Matters and affairs will be fortunate for the individual but on a smaller scale. It brings good fortune in the form of love for something or someone, and brings a much brighter personality especially to one who has a dour expression. This will occur even though a restrictive planet may be in conjunction. The native will find good things coming his/her way but always in a minor way. Any winnings in games of chance will be on a small scale and not of great proportions.

Part of Fortune in the Second House

There is a benefit through a financial gain with this placement. This is an appropriate time for a financial investment that will bring the person a small return. There will be fortune in games of chance, financial affairs, and material possessions. However, the native should be advised that it is not an appropriate time to purchase expensive objects or costly material goods. This position brings fortune through money and all matters of one's personal financial affairs, but always in a small way. Although this can be a person who tends to spend too much money, there will not be the opportunity nor the resources to make large purchases at this time.

Part of Fortune in the Third House

The individual will find enjoyment with relatives. One will be happy communicating directly with relatives, having conversations about relatives, or taking journeys with relatives. This is one placement where the native will deal more with relatives than at any other time in life, no matter what other planetary effects may exist at this time or in later years. The person will incorporate relatives in travel, communication, and all matters related to this house. This position brings joy in a small way to family activities, such as family reunions.

Although this is a fortunate time for a literary work to be started, it must have a relative involved in some way, either writing with a relative, about a relative, through a relative, or journeys with a relative. The writing will, in some way, incorporate relatives. This is the only placement where the native truly enjoys being involved with relatives.

Part of Fortune in the Fourth House

The individual enjoys being at home more often and for longer periods than in the past. This is a fortunate time for social activities in the home. For the native who has had a poor relationship with the dominant one of the family, this is the time to develop a better relationship with that person even though it may be short lived.

This is a good time to spend small amounts on repairs to the home; to improve the home or real estate, to acquire adjacent property, or to invest in real estate in a small way. It is a time to look for a bargain in the purchase of real estate.

Part of Fortune in the Fifth House

Joy is brought to all affairs related to this placement. One who is generally irritated with children will be delighted to be around children.

The native will fall in love many times during this transit and not just with other persons—falling in love with love. It must be stressed that the native will fall in love many times with sports, speculation, children, entertainment, or other matters of this house. If the native intends to speculate, he or she should be advised to speculate on a small scale and not get carried away with grand schemes. Betting at the tracks will not bring the person large sums; therefore, bets should be in small amounts so that smaller winnings will be expected.

Part of Fortune in the Sixth House
There is pleasure at work and a learning process with respect to health. The native will try other remedies for certain ailments, such as herbal medicines or natural healings. There will be pleasure in little things, especially those things dealing with health. One will try to find solutions for health problems that afflict small animals, developing new diets, natural foods, and alternative medicines. It is a good time for the person to deal with small animals in general, and there will be involvement with more than one animal. The individual will find joy as a volunteer for the humane society or other organizations dealing with animals, and the native should be encouraged to get involved with groups devoted to animals.

There will be joy on a small scale related to all matters of this house. It brings joy to the workplace and in little things the native finds beneficial, which would then be passed on to others. This is an opportune time to write articles with respect to health if the individual is so inclined.

Part of Fortune in the Seventh House
If the native is involved in litigation, it is a good time to settle with a plaintiff for a smaller amount. It is fortunate for a small compromise as this placement is beneficial in a small way, and thus work to the person's advantage. The same will be true if the native is the plaintiff in a lawsuit. The native should be advised to choose a smaller settlement through compromise, and should not go for the entire amount. Those involved in litigation become extremely emotional and it is difficult for them to accept less, but they will be much happier settling the lawsuit for less than they expected to receive. It is a time to be diplomatic.

More than likely, this is the time the native finds a new mate, and it will bring happiness on a small scale. One could also find enjoyment with an old partner or a relationship that brings joy. The native will be before the public, engaging in outside activities with the new mate or a renewed relationship. There will be more social events and entertainment than in the past.

Part of Fortune in the Eighth House

There native will enjoy funerals, and be the person others would like to have in attendance because the individual will have the ability to make the grief stricken feel better.

There will be an interest in the occult, and the native will find a number of sexual adventures occurring during this time. The sexual encounters will be numerous and exciting; however, they will be on a small scale. The adventures will not produce a great romantic relationship, but simple little romances.

There will be matters related to insurance, legacies, other people's money and petty crime. The native with this placement will be a good individual to employ in order to settle problems with an inheritance. A person with this position who is involved in petty theft will get away with their crimes as long as they are petty in nature. It will be pleasurable for them; that is, a sick pleasure during the solar return year. However, if one engages in major crimes, the good fortune is lost and the native will be caught.

This is a good time for the native to have a psychic reading. The reading will be enjoyed and helpful information will be received. It could also be the person who gets pleasure from calling every advertised psychic line. If the native is a psychic, the number of clients will increase but the readings will be shorter. The reason for this is that there will be fewer questions and the responses will be shorter and precise.

Part of Fortune in the Ninth House

The spiritual and philosophical are involved with this placement, together with all affairs of this house. A college student with this position will change the major. One will enjoy seeking out courtrooms, attorneys, professors, and other professional areas. Plans will be made for a long distance journey, but the journey will be short; or it would be a long distance journey over a short period of time. Foreign travel will be short either in time or distance. Travel may be a requirement for academic studies. It is a fortunate time to seek out other universities if the native wishes to change. In any event, it will be an active time for the native.

This is a good time for a politician to marry or to take a journey and have someone else pay the cost. This will be for only a short period. The native will find joy in researching spiritual and religious matters, but it would not be a good time to write a major thesis on any subject. Small articles will be fortunate, but a novel will not. The native with this placement should be advised to have a good time and not to worry as long as moral grounds are maintained.

Part of Fortune in the Tenth House

This is fortunate for career, but in a small way. It could be a small increase, promotion, or just a pat on the back. The individual will enjoy the career more at this time than heretofore.

The individual should be encouraged to work with the less fortunate as a volunteer, or with the government in some way, and will enjoy doing these things at this time.

This is the year for the individual to find joy in discovering other cultures and races, and will enjoy seeking out information on pigs and goats or farming, depending on how the individual is living life. For a farmer, this is a good time to learn about pig farming, or one who has a political background could take up the cause of the farmer. The placement depends upon the influence of this house in the natal chart.

Part of Fortune in the Eleventh House

The native spends much more time with friends, and will have the extra money necessary to socialize with them. This opportunity would not have been there before, but this is the year that makes it happen.

It will not be necessary at this time to ask for a raise in salary as there will be a small increase without asking for it. There will be joys, but on a small scale, that will involve friendships, income, hopes and wishes, and little fortunate occurrences that will come up in life. If the parson is so inclined, this is the time to accept a position of leadership in an organization.

Part of Fortune in the Twelfth House

The native will be fortunate on a small scale. For example, he or she will be forewarned of a secret enemy who is seeking to hurt him/her in some way; thus, one could avoid any type of coming confrontation.

An individual with an illness will discover it is minor and can be taken care of with no serious consequences. It is a time for the individual to volunteer to help in a hospital or institution.

This placement is a lucky point that helps the individual out of difficulties. A petty thief caught in the act will be freed by a court. However, this would not occur with one who is involved in a major crime. This placement, in a small way, brings fortune out of adversity,

Individuals with this placement who wish to develop their psychic ability should keep their efforts on a small scale, working with it a little at a time. Care should be taken in developing psychic ability, including obtaining the services of a person who has been proven reliable. This is the time for the native to be manipulated and sent down the wrong path.

This is a fortunate position for psychic dreams, creativity and inspiration, but on a small scale. There will be brief periods when the individual can see a former life through dreams or visions when in a dreamlike state. There will be only small glimpses of the former life, but they will be accurate.

South Node—Negative Attitudes

Individuals are induced to develop a negative attitude to those matters of the house placement. It is a position individuals bring upon themselves, and it is strictly a mental attitude they have chosen. Because of their own doing, it can be overcome when and if they choose to do so. Its energies consist of vocal complaints, but with little or no action taking place.

South Node in the First House

The individual has little confidence in self or outlook throughout the solar year, awakening each day and being depressed. The native does not feel inspired to go about the daily routine, and there is difficulty in starting the day. The person feels everything is adverse with respect to early morning activities or with anything new or different to start the day. This is an unfortunate placement for the person since the feeling is not readily understood, The native will constantly complain about his/her surroundings, causing many to avoid the native.

South Node in the Second House

There is dissatisfaction with material possessions. The native has the feeling there is not enough of what is needed, causing frustration. The native feels he or she is unable to put enough money away, bringing unhappiness and a lack of confidence with money and material possessions, as well as complaining about the financial situation. There is no inclination to invest money in anything during the solar return year.

South Node in the Third House

There will be a constant complaint about a relative, or relatives, and the native will dread being involved with relatives at this time. The native will tend to avoid taking trips, especially with relatives. When communicating with others the native displays a dour personality, and sometimes a foul mouth. There will be difficulty in writing or communicating at this time, but the native will be learning to work through this, even though it is difficult. Most relatives will avoid the native, but in all likelihood there will be one who will give the person the most difficulty.

South Node in the Fourth House

The native will avoid the home, not wish to spend much time in the home, or stay away to avoid involvement with a dominant parent. This can be the person who travels frequently and will not be in the home during this time. This is not the time to plant or cultivate since the native will be unhappy at this time with his/her environment, wishing to move but being unable to do so because of frequent travels or other matters that keep the native away from home. At other times, the individual will look for an excuse to stay away from home. In any event, being away from home will not be a bother. This is a good position for the person who has to travel for extended periods, since there would be little concern or worry about the home.

South Node in the Fifth House

The individual will complain about poor luck with respect to games of chance, feeling like the last person to win. There will be no enjoyment with children, and this is the year there will be difficulty in finding a love interest. No relationship at this time would appeal to the person, and there will be no place of amusement or entertainment that will be satisfactory. This will be the one who is miserable when everyone else is having a good time. They native will even avoid athletics or sports. However, it is a good position for a couch potato.

South Node in the Sixth House

There will be dissatisfaction with employment with this position. The native will be disgruntled with employment even though in the recent past there was great pleasure with work. This is the time when the native feels nothing seems to work out right in the workplace, even to the point where the job makes the native ill. It is possible the individual could become ill because of unhappiness surrounding employment.

Animals will be a problem because of allergies caused by the individual's mental attitude, or work will be missed due to worry over the health of animals. A miserable time can be expected with everything related to work, pets, health, and other matters of this house.

South Node in the Seventh House
There will be dissatisfaction with marriage. The individual will constantly find fault with the public if involved with the public in any capacity. Thus, one will avoid the public and public matters. The native will complain about marriage and the marriage of others, and have a negative attitude toward all marriages. This is a good time to divorce since marriage is the scene of constant complaints.

This is not be a good time for the individual to be involved in litigation because of a negative attitude and vocal complaints toward the justice system and most everyone in the courtroom. This could be the native's undoing. The native should be advised to avoid litigation at all costs. Unfortunately, however, this is the person who will not listen and thus becomes involved in a legal quagmire.

South Node in the Eighth House
There will be complaints with respect to insurance, the occult, or the person's sex life. In all likelihood, it will be a complaint with respect to the sex life voiced to others or a complaint directed to the partner. There will be complaints directed at the occult, sex in general, crime, insurance companies, funerals, and cemeteries. The complaints would not be based on reality, for the most part.

Complaints can involve funerals that the person tries to avoid during this solar year. However, it will be a vocal complaint and in the end, the native will still have to attend one or more funerals while exhibiting unhappiness.

South Node in the Ninth House
There will be discontentment with the individual's church, religion, studies, philosophy, and journeys. A journey would be miserable at this time. There could be a change in travel agents several times during the year.

This is not a good year for the individual to complete studies since the mind will wander. The native will feel like moving on to something else, and will find fault with a professor or course of study if in college. There could be a change in philosophy or denigration of that which the native had been taught throughout life. In a way, this would be rather fortunate because the individual could be one who was extremely dogmatic about a philosophy or religion and now finds that what he or she was taught to believe is no longer an inspiration or truth.

South Node in the Tenth House

Unhappiness besets the individual with respect to career, a superior, government, business, the poor; welfare, or a parent. It is an attitude that will pass after the solar year so that the native should be advised to hang on to what he or she has until it is over. There will be difficulties working for, or with, a government or corporation at this time; thus, any contractual agreements will bring about many complaints. The individual should be advised not to change career while this placement is in effect.

South Node in the Eleventh House

There will be dissatisfaction with friends and income from career. It will not be a fortunate time to ask for an increase in salary. The individual will have a feeling of despair when it comes to hopes and wishes. This is not the year to be involved with an organization since the native's negative attitude can bring about rumors and disorganization within a group. The native could start a rumor about a friend that stirs up problems within a fellowship or an association. The negative attitude will be in the mind of the person but it can bring about long term problems, such as burning bridges with friends, and thus making it difficult to make amends at a later time.

South Node in the Twelfth House

There will be hatred directed to the enemies of the native, who will confront them in a way that would not have been considered prior to this solar year. This is a placement that could place the individual into a harmful situation. The native could talk to the wrong people and thus be in serious trouble. The individual should be advised not to become involved with those on the lower side of life or those involved with illegal activities.

The person will be miserable in a hospital or institution of any kind. He or she will complain about the criminal system and its employees or anyone connected with the system. However, they are vocal complaints without any meaningful action.

A psychic with this placement will lose confidence in the ability to channel and will consider turning to other interests or a different occult study. This placement can turn the individual back to organized religion. This depends on the strength and will of the individual. Attitude and lack of confidence is a self-imposed misery.

Those giving psychic readings at this time will continue to receive correct information; however, they will feel they are not correctly passing it on to their clients. They could also have a negative attitude about clients when giving readings, and should be advised that it is a self-imposed unrealistic attitude and to work toward establishing the confidence of the past.

North Node—Positive Attitudes

This placement brings a positive attitude and confidence with a little bit of good fortune. It can be considered a lucky charm since it is always a benefit and bestows upon the individual a positive outlook throughout the solar year.

North Node in the First House

The native develops a perky attitude at this time. There will be confidence within and the feeling that one should push him\herself to do those things he or she previously was afraid to try or venture into. It is fortunate for beginnings and the individual will find that he or she enjoys the beginning of most everything. There is a positive attitude and the native looks forward to each day. It is fortunate for all new endeavors.

North Node in the Second House

There is greater confidence in financial matters and possessions. The native will begin to like a banking connection and feel satisfied with possessions. There will be a feeling of happiness over possessions acquired. This is the time the native will wish to invest a small amount of money which will prove beneficial at a later time. This is the position of confidence so that any investment made will be on a small scale and in small increments. The individual will not plunge into an investment with all of his/her money. Investments made at a prior time will pay dividends and the individual feels quite confident that the correct investment decision was made at that time. The native does not overspend with this position despite of their confidence in money matters, unless an expansive planet is also positioned in this house.

North Node in the Third House

The individual enjoys short travels and may even find someone to go along, such as a relative or a good communicator who will make the trip enjoyable. The individual will enjoy using a citizen's band radio while traveling in order to speak to others on the road. A cellular telephone may be purchased to help break the monotony while traveling. The native will feel much more confident speaking to others in this manner. In prior years, the person may not have had the confidence or the opportunity to travel, but now can do so without worry.

This is an opportune time to start a manuscript or begin some type of creative writing. The person will have more energy and confidence to begin such a project. Writing will come much easier at this time.

North Node in the Fourth House

Happiness and confidence in all affairs of this house can be expected. The native will enjoy being involved with a dominant parent as he or she will have a new outlook toward that parent. There will be satisfaction with the home and a desire to do those things that will make it even more enjoyable. This is the time when the person receives gifts for the home from those invited into their home or buys certain articles to improve the home in some way.

The individual who hesitated in the past to look for a home or real estate investments has the confidence at this time to do so. If a home is owned, it will bring more confidence in the purchase previously made.

This is a time when the native feels confident in bringing another person into the home. Prior to this, there may have been fear in allowing another to live in the home. However, in spite of the confidence, much care should be used for the reason that this position of confidence and luck is only for the solar year.

North Node in the Fifth House
The native will begin enjoying life more at this time. This shows the beginning of a love affair or a love affair with the entertainment industry, sports, or children. The native will have a favorable feeling for a child who had been destructive or difficult to handle.

If the individual is involved in a love relationship, it will bring a new spark into the relationship. The native will appreciate what he or she has in life, such as the environment, loved ones, and children. It is a good time to enjoy life and what it has to offer.

North Node in the Sixth House
There will be confidence in the workplace and in health with this placement. Those that have been constantly worrying about health and work will welcome this position. This could be one who had a difficult time with a recent illness but now feels confident that wellness will come. There is an interest in alternative medicine or natural health products, and the native will have more interest in herbs and other natural remedies. It brings confidence in alternative methods of healing that can benefit the native more than by following a physician's orders.

This is an excellent time to bring a pet into the home. It will help a person through an illness or depression. A change of attitude and confidence brought about through enjoyment of a pet will allay any worry about health. It is an excellent time to work with animals. This placement does not eliminate a disease, but it does bring confidence to the individual to seek other methods of healing.

The individual who has been unhappy with employment will now find that many of the problems have been corrected either through the removal of certain individuals or improvement in work environment.

North Node in the Seventh House
There will be confidence and enjoyment in working with the public. The individual will be more outgoing and will socialize much more during this solar year. There will be confidence in taking on a partner or a partnership of some kind. This is the person who did not previously have confidence in the partner or did not particularly like socializing. Confidence will return at this time and marriage will feel good.

There will be more involvement with contracts and law, but it will be on a minor level. Since this is a strong house position, there could be too much confidence with this placement, resulting in the native being in an uncomfortable or difficult situation. However, overall it will be a very positive year. It is the year that many choose to renew their wedding vows.

At this time the native enjoys courtroom dramas, reading about the law, or watching programs pertaining to the law, marriage, partnerships, and public matters.

North Node in the Eighth House
Individuals with this transit will find themselves enjoying life. They will enjoy sex with added confidence in their sexuality. The individual will experiment with sex in general and with sexual positions, and is sexually motivated by psychic or sexual experiences that were psychically related.

There will be joy in dealing with legacies, inheritance, insurance, research, death, cemeteries, and underworld matters. The native will enjoy murder stories and investigative matters. There will be a positive feeling with respect to the physical beauty of cemeteries with the many flowers, peace and serenity. This is a period of time when the native has more confidence in death and dying as he or she begins to overcome some of the fears of the past. It is an especially good position for one who has a terminal illness for he or she will find solace and comfort in learning about the forthcoming transition from a physical to a spiritual life.

North Node in the Ninth House

With this placement the native finds more confidence in foreigners, foreign lands, foreign investments and the professional class of people, along with the feeling of being in a professional job or career. It gives one a boost in attitude toward professionalism and in continuing the education in some field or course of study.

The native will feel he or she must find the opportunity to travel more. However, any travelling done will not be for an extended period of time. It could possibly be a cruise, a business conference, or a short trip to some foreign country depending on the financial condition.

Confidence in one's spiritual or religious heritage is renewed with this placement. There is a restoration of faith in spirituality and that spiritual beliefs will guide him/her safely through life.

North Node in the Tenth House

The native will consistently talk about the career, how it was chosen, and how all the right moves were made. The native becomes rather egotistical about his/her standing with respect to career matters. It is also the time for the person to become more involved with the government, which can include assisting a politician running for office. This brings confidence involving governmental matters that relate to welfare, bankruptcy, taxes, and other programs of government. The native who is not involved personally in any of these areas will still feel confident that government programs are working better now than they had in the past.

This is the time that the native reunites with a parent for he or she is able to overcome a lack of confidence in dealing with that parent. It opens the door for discussion of those serious events that had occurred but were never fully discussed or explained to satisfaction.

The native will be inclined to accept a better job offer because of confidence in the ability to handle the position. Sheer enthusiasm may bring about some additional responsibility related to the present job that would bring about a promotion. The native could also have the confidence and desire to take on a second job or career to supplement the income.

North Node in the Eleventh House
With this placement, the native spends more time with friends and organizations with which there was no involvement prior to this time. This is a renewal of friendships or a desire to visit those friends not seen for a long time. There is more confidence in earning ability and in hopes and wishes. The native feels that those things set in motion will open up new avenues of income.

This is a period of socializing and in renewing friendships that can have long lasting benefits. Friendships can be very powerful for the purpose of reaching goals. With this placement, there is confidence and a positive attitude in running for an office in a large organization where strong friendships can be made, thereby helping the native realize some or all hopes and wishes.

North Node in the Twelfth House
This placement has a dual effect. The native may consume more alcoholic beverages than before, and make frequent visits to places where alcohol and drugs are available. This can incline the person to take drugs or a combination of alcohol and drugs, including prescription medication. The native will feel confident that everything will turn out well with health, spouse, and others in life. An-

other side to this placement finds the native volunteering his or her services to a hospital or other institution to experience the sorrows of others. In this way, one will appreciate his or her own situation and what he or she has in life.

There will be a change in attitude toward those the native felt were secret enemies, and will take a positive approach to those considered enemies and thus have a better feeling toward them. In most instances, however, the native will find out later that he or she was being undermined by them all along.

This is the psychic house and the native will begin to develop psychic ability or be inspired by the spiritual, being pulled in both directions at the same time. There may be involvement in working with psychic matters, but at the same time there could be excessive socializing and drinking more than usual. It could be that the person experiences one or the other, but in all likelihood the individual will probably become involved with a little of both.

One who is psychic may give readings in bars or for people taking illegal drugs. On the other hand, the native could help the unfortunate in hospitals or institutions. This placement pulls in both directions. Yet there is another side to this that involves this Node in Virgo. The opposite Node is in Pisces, the sign ruling this house. The effect will deter the native from drugs, alcohol, hospitals, and institutions. This person will try to bring health into a sick environment, but avoid hospitals for fear of contracting a disease.

Persephone—Sweetness and Light

The planet ruling the sign Libra has yet to be found in this age. It is only goodness and light, the sweetest of all planets. It represents the beauty of Venus but not its indulgences. It brings sweetness and light, creative ability, shyness, innocence, frivolity, and naivete wherever placed in the natal or solar return chart.

To determine the sign placement, this planet will be a maximum of sixty degrees from the Sun; that is, its sign position will be the same as the Sun sign, in the sign before the Sun sign, or in the sign after. Its sign position can easily be determined by the interpretation of its effect in the houses of the solar return chart.

Persephone in the First House

It will bring a sweetness to the personality for the solar year, but it is also a very good position to have natally. The individual who has a natal dour placement, such as a Capricorn Ascendant or Saturn in this house, will have an unexpected turn of events. The native with this placement will make small gestures of kindness toward other people, but it will also bring a shyness and a naivete to the personality. This is the planet of sweetness, but the person can also be a little naive when involved with earthly affairs. The year will see the individual becoming a little shy, a little bashful, or a little naive in the approach to many things during the solar year.

Persephone in the Second House

This is not a favorable position for investments or banking. Pleasure will be derived from spending money on creative matters, such as art, crafts, flowers, or simply bringing bits of joy to others. It can be one who will be creative with respect to finances, but naive in dealings with such matters. Love will extend to music, singing, and musical instruments, and the native will sing frequently or discover a more lyrical quality to the speaking voice. This will not include singing or performing for the public, for this is not a position of an extrovert. The individual will perform for his or her own amusement—singing along with the radio or playing an instrument.

Persephone in the Third House

This is a good position for tolerating relatives if there was no prior communication with relatives. The relatives will be more personable so the native will be able to accept them in a much easier frame of mind.

There will be a lyrical quality to communications, together with a little naivete. There will be a lyrical and poetic quality to the speaking voice at this time or a melodic way of communicating. The native may speak in rhymes or reminisce with respect to songs of the past. This is a person who finds a naive attraction to poetry. However, it will be poetry of sweetness, freshness, and love. The native will have desire to write poetry for his or her own pleasure. This is the house of limitations for this planet, more so than any other house.

Persephone in the Fourth House
Love and happiness for the home and family is indicated. A person who did not previously enjoy the home because of problems will bring some brightness, love, joy, and an uplift in the emotions. The native will enjoy bringing a little music, art, and creativity into the home environment; however, the native will be somewhat naive in connection with these matters.

Any artistic endeavors by the native will not be publicly displayed. The native will bring a lighter and more artistic quality to the home, but with a type of naivete and innocence. Art objects or flower arrangements, for example, will be sweet, simple, and not grandiose. The native who did not previously enjoy the home will bring brightness, joy, and the finer things of life into the home, but only on a small scale.

Persephone in the Fifth House
It brings a new love to the individual, but it would be more of an infatuation than true love—an innocent love of another. The native will feel he or she is truly in love, when in reality it will simply be an innocent infatuation. By bringing this upon him/herself, a broken heart could result. If the native is young, in all probability it would be the first love.

There will be an innocent love of children, and the native will find pleasure in taking children to finer places of entertainment. It will be entertainment of an innocent nature. They will see the innocence and have a healthy attitude toward sports, amusements, children, entertainment, and all things related to this house.

Persephone in the Sixth House

Individuals will find themselves helping those who are ill. They will find delight in helping people and animals in the workplace, surroundings, or where they may be needed, with alternative and natural methods of healing. They will be delighted with their pets and wild creatures for they will find innocence in all things. However, if the individual is so naive as to not use caution around unfriendly, wild, and roaming animals, there is the possibility of contracting a serious illness. There is a great deal of naivete in the quest to help what the native believes are innocent and helpless creatures.

The work environment will be more delightful at this time. The individual will enjoy being at the place of employment, even to the point of volunteering to work in an area where previously there was little or no interest.

Persephone in the Seventh House

This is the strongest placement for this planet, and excellent position because it has a powerful effect in this house. It takes away some of the naivete, and brings to the native a much stronger and confident nature. There will be much creativity in the life of the individual, who will enjoy the cultural side of life, such as classical orchestra concerts, museums, art exhibits, poetry groups, the opera, and all those things concerning the fine arts. This is the time the native will want to buy and play a musical instrument, or purchase music and those things that bring cultural activities into the life.

There is a strong tendency for partnerships and marriage at this time. The native will take the view that partnerships and marriage are very important. The person will have a strong tendency to be married, and will take the attitude that marriage is good and this is the year to be married. There will be no way for others to convince the native not to get married because of the strong effect of this planet in this house during the solar return year. It is at home in this house and thus becomes the best indicator for marriage. The native could be a perfect partner for someone, but the possibility exists that it may last only a year!

Persephone in the Eighth House

It would be good to have the individual with this placement at a funeral service for he or she would say only nice things about the deceased. The native will bring food to the family of the deceased, donate money to a cause, or volunteer to help at the service in some way. The native will be inclined to pursue all areas surrounding death. It will be a rather naive approach to death, but sincere. The native will feel that by bringing a little brightness and happiness during this difficult time, it will be of great help to the loved ones of the deceased. It is all related to the affairs of the dead,

The native will enjoy the occult but more in a lighthearted way, finding it tolerable and interesting, but not dwelling too heavily into it at this time The native will more likely be involved in helping others dealing with an estate, an insurance policy problem, or something having to do with the affairs of the deceased.

This is a shy planet in the house of sex. The individual will think sex is not a noble act and will not wish to sink to that level. Rather, the native will seek to bring the sex act up to his/her level. The attitude would be naive towards sex; therefore, the native will not be consumed by it. The favorite and most often heard response will be that sex is reserved for marriage. However, it could just be an attitude for the year which can easily change at the conclusion of the solar return.

Persephone in the Ninth House

The individual will be a constant philosopher for the year, quoting certain philosophical material or speaking in little philosophical rhymes such as "the early bird catches the worm." It is innocence and brightness, but not true philosophy. The native will find a true interest in philosophy, but will take it lightly.

This is the period when the individual in school will be delighted with the academic surroundings, but will not complete courses as the tendency will be to skim the surface. Although the native would be delighted to be in a profession, he or she will not be able to complete the studies. The native will enjoy the creative arts in school, but in all likelihood will not accomplish much during the solar year. The native will have fun in the academic environment, but will not take studies seriously.

Persephone in the Tenth House
The individual will contemplate changing careers at this time, feeling almost anything can be done despite the fact that background or experience in other areas is lacking.

The effect of this planet is best when the native is helping the less fortunate. There is a sweetness and a naivete when the individual is involved in volunteer work with respect to the poor, the sick, the elderly, and others who need help. The native will not be able to correct problems of the unfortunate but will enjoy helping in a less substantial way such as working for a short time behind a food line or passing out toys to children. There will be an innocence and sweetness to these endeavors and others will enjoy their presence. Most people, however, will find them humorous.

Persephone in the Eleventh House
There will be involvement with many different areas pertaining to organizations or groups. The native will volunteer to help with golf tournaments, for example, or social and charitable organizations. The native will believe he or she has many good but innocent ideas, but they will be of a light nature and without any real substance. The native will do well with the social activities of an organization. There will be a unique approach to most things, but this is someone who should not be put in charge of anything that would be exceptionally difficult.

The native's hopes and wishes at this time are to be invited to join a certain organization, that income will be enhanced by membership in a certain organization, or that involvement with a certain group or organization will be beneficial.

Persephone in the Twelfth House

The individual should be warned to stay away from those on the lower side of life. This planet brings a naivete in all of the houses, and with this house placement the native will not recognize the dangers ahead.

It is best that the person use this position to volunteer services at a hospital, prison, or other institutions, but the native should not become too involved with any of the employees or other individuals in the institutions. Because of the native's naivete and innocence in this environment, he or she can be taken in easily. For example, the individual can be convinced of the innocence of a prisoner, and foolishly spend time and money in an attempt to free the prisoner or to provide for his or her needs. Others with this placement will marry a notorious convict, for in their own naive way they believe they can change the person to be a fine spouse and a law abiding citizen. The native can be oblivious to many of the matters pertaining to this house placement.

This is the year the native becomes inspired by religion. Instead of simply going through the motions of attending services, the native will feel the need to seek a higher purpose in life through the chosen religion. The native will be extremely naive during this time and should use care not to be fooled by what has been accepted as religious truths.

There is a naivete with respect to secret enemies. The individual will delight in bringing happiness to all, including corrupt and evil individuals. This can turn out to be fortunate for the native since enemies will not believe that anyone could be so naive and innocent, and thus will leave the native alone.

For additional information on Persephone and Vulcan and their influence in the natal chart, consult the books *The Lives You Live as Revealed in the Heavens, Uranus Neptune Pluto: The Spiritual Trinity* by Ted George, and the *North & South Nodes: Guideposts of the Spirit*, by Cynthia Bohannon.

Vulcan (Chiron)—The Great Healer

Named Chiron by its discoverer, but better known as Hephaestus in Greek mythology and Vulcan in the Roman version, it is the ruler of the sign Virgo, This god in mythology was portrayed as the lame god, deformed and ugly, who was cast out of heaven by his mother Hera. Hence, it was lost to those of earth in the Age of Pisces, its opposite sign.

It is a child of the Moon and it travels with the Moon; thus, it is located either in the same sign as the Moon sign, in the sign before the Moon sign, or in the sign after. Consider the sign position, in addition to the house, when interpreting its effect for the solar year, as it will signify where its health properties are active.

This planet is the great healer and it has a very positive and influential effect on health and all matters pertaining to health; not with respect to illness, but in terms of being healthy. It is the opposite planet to Neptune in the area of disease. This is the planet that brings about health, and its interest concerns all matters related to the natural approach to healing, which is totally opposite to the negative influences of Neptune with its chemicals and drugs for healing.

It is a very beneficial planet and should not be categorized as a malefic simply because it also rules the work environment. It is one's work and a positive attitude for accomplishment that brings good health.

Vulcan in the First House

This is an excellent placement for this planet. This is the individual with a healthy mind, attitude, and a positive outlook, who will have a great interest in dealing with those areas pertaining to health. Look to the sign placement as to where the native pursues health, such as exercise and sports if placed in the sign Leo. The individual will have a healthy childhood, recovering quickly from any childhood illness. It is a very good placement for one who has not had a healthy past or who may now be bedridden. It will benefit them through a positive attitude toward illness and a desire to seek some form of exercise or natural healing.

Vulcan in the Second House

The native will have a healthy outlook on his/her financial situation and material possessions, which will relieve stress, especially for those who worry greatly about the financial condition. Those who came through a difficult financial period without causing harm to themselves or others will find they are now being rewarded by having this placement for the solar year.

The individual may elect to invest in areas of natural health, such as the holistic approach to healing, herbs, and natural cures. However, one who has an unhealthy attitude toward money could apply this position in a negative way. Aspects must always be considered when defining this placement. For the most part, this position indicates health and the positive benefits of health and attitude when dealing with finances, both physically and mentally. Those who carry many negative earthbound influences such as an addiction will find that this planet brings relief.

Vulcan in the Third House

The native will be inclined to write about or discuss herbs for mental or physical health. This will not be dealing with illness or hospitals, but it can involve the subject of making hospitals healthier. The person will express health in some way during the solar year—reading many articles about health, or communicating, expressing, or traveling to express knowledge of health issues involving both the home and work environments. The native may write an article with respect to research in plants that grow wild along highways and fields and how the plants can provide many health benefits.

Vulcan in the Fourth House

The individual will bring health to an unhealthy home environment, either in the form of peace or through health, mediation, or harmony and balance. Health can be a broad term when related to this placement. The person may bring a positive attitude to a dysfunctional family by applying a more regimented and healthier energy to the home. The native may feel he or she should go to the homes of others in an effort to straighten out a dysfunctional and unhealthy environment. The native will be influential in bringing about a healthy home, a clean house, or bringing about an entirely new and positive attitude to his/her way of life.

Vulcan in the Fifth House

This brings a healthy attitude toward love, children, and all matters of this house. The individual could choose to work with children in order to help them grow up in a healthier environment, or influence the diet of children or loved ones. The native will have a positive influence on children and by so doing, it will also benefit the individual. However, the person can become somewhat dogmatic about this and thus bring about negative repercussions. It would be advisable for those who have this placement not to become obsessive in their efforts to make their influence strongly felt.

This placement can bring a healthy lover to the individual, or cause the native to work harder with respect to a love relationship. It brings a healthy attitude toward a lover, children, entertainment, sports and all matters of this house if the individual will work to achieve this goal. This is a natural position for this house so the individual should be cautioned not to become obsessive with these matters.

Vulcan in the Sixth House

A healthy work environment is brought to the individual. It can bring a desire for the person to find employment in the health field that is not related to illness, such as someone who attempts to make the surroundings healthier. This does bring a healthier attitude to the workplace if the native did not have a good attitude about it in the past. The native may begin to bring healthier food and drink items into the workplace, which would benefit everyone. The individual will feel happier and healthier as there will be a better attitude about work and surroundings. This placement does bring about very good benefits in some way.

Vulcan in the Seventh House

A person who works in the health field will bring many new ideas to the public, and attract many people because of discoveries related to health. This is a good position for an individual to promote the benefits of health, a healthy attitude, and a positive work environment. It can bring a partner who has a great influence or a background in healing, health, mental health, herbs, or holistic medicine. The partner could be working in the health field or have access to the public for lectures on health related subjects. The person can experience a healthy relationship or a healthy partner for the solar year. It is a good placement for travel, and lectures about the healing benefits of herbs and a positive approach to healing.

If the individual has a political background, this could be the person who attempts to get certain legislation passed with respect to the elimination or the placement of warning labels on certain unhealthy and dangerous products being sold to the public.

Vulcan in the Eighth House

There is a healthier attitude toward the occult, together with a healthier attitude toward the insurance industry. This is a good placement for the individual to influence changes in the health field through insurance companies that deal with illnesses and other problems. Those with this position who work within the insurance industry could help bring about changes in the working environment by demanding more physicals before issuing policies, more healthy attitudes, and more effort to keep their policyholders healthier and living longer.

The native will acquire a healthier attitude toward the occult and all metaphysical areas. However, it does bring to the native a change of attitude toward burials in that the person will approach the subject as being an unhappy and unpleasant method of interring the body. The native will feel that burials are not happy situations and that there should be a different and healthier attitude with respect to death and dying.

Vulcan in the Ninth House

The individual in some way will study subjects with respect to health, herbs, psychology, or mental health, but not necessarily at a university. The native will have a great interest in these subjects, and may even decide to teach or seek employment in these areas. If the individual is a student at a university, he or she will bring a healthy attitude to the campus. With leadership abilities and strength of character, the individual can make changes to benefit the students, especially if the person has political connections in order to bring it about.

Vulcan in the Tenth House

The native will feel that the government is not treating those in poverty well; and that the poor do not eat well and do not have good dietary habits. An individual with this placement in some type of authority can make beneficial changes with respect to the poor.

The native may decide to enter a career or a job related to health, and may wish to dedicate his/her life to improve the lives of the less fortunate, The person can bring about a healthier approach to government or the chosen career, and will be influenced in these areas either in a small way or on a large scale.

The individual could choose to sell vitamins, herbs, or other health items out of the home, and learn about health through this endeavor. This would be ideal for the person who is drawing subsistence from the government, as he or she could earn additional income and learn how to stay healthy.

Vulcan in the Eleventh House

The person may decide to seek medical counsel and go into therapy in order to have a better attitude and healthier friends, and make healthier choices. The native may join organizations that deal with health or a health spa, or sell health products or exercise equipment to supplement income. The native may join a certain organization or group simply to become acquainted with their methods and ideas.

One who is in the health field will find a way to introduce creative ideas to others, such as developing a new exercise program or equipment for adults and children. The person may develop a fun way for children to exercise in order to stay healthy. This could be done for material gain, but the native will also benefit by becoming health conscious.

Vulcan in the Twelfth House

This is a good position for the individual to do something about correcting the diet in hospitals, believing that a person who is hospitalized is confined in an unhealthy environment. One working in this field will tend to bring about revolutionary ideas to make hospitals healthier. This will be challenging, but one with this placement can bring it forth with determination.

The native will feel that health inspections of taverns, restaurants, night clubs, and other places serving the public are not adequate and will report unsanitary conditions to the proper government agency. This is a very good placement for those who wish to clean up their own environment.

This position cannot be used in a negative way. For the person who is an alcoholic or who uses illegal drugs, this is the best time to join Alcoholics Anonymous or seek drug rehabilitation. This is the year the native will not enjoy indulgences as much at frequently visited places.

"Astronomy can enlarge our knowledge
of the universe, but the presence of
astrology will continue to be regarded as
the most important part in the interpretation of life."

Ted George

Solar Return Graph
A Chronology of the Annual Solar Returns

Year_____ |___|___|		|___|___|		|___|___|			|___|___|		

	H	S		H	S		H	S		H	S	
Sun	|	|	|	|	|	|	|	|	|	|	|	|
Venus	|	|	|	|	|	|	|	|	|	|	|	|
Mercury	|	|	|	|	|	|	|	|	|	|	|	|
Moon	|	|	|	|	|	|	|	|	|	|	|	|
Mars	|	|	|	|	|	|	|	|	|	|	|	|
Jupiter	|	|	|	|	|	|	|	|	|	|	|	|
Saturn	|	|	|	|	|	|	|	|	|	|	|	|
Uranus	|	|	|	|	|	|	|	|	|	|	|	|
Neptune	|	|	|	|	|	|	|	|	|	|	|	|
Pluto	|	|	|	|	|	|	|	|	|	|	|	|
Lilith	|	|	|	|	|	|	|	|	|	|	|	|
Part Fortune	|	|	|	|	|	|	|	|	|	|	|	|
South Node	|	|	|	|	|	|	|	|	|	|	|	|
North Node	|	|	|	|	|	|	|	|	|	|	|	|
Persephone	|	|	|	|	|	|	|	|	|	|	|	|
Vulcan	|	|	|	|	|	|	|	|	|	|	|	|
Ascendant	|	|	|	|	|	|	|	|	|	|	|	|

H=House S=Sign
Use sign symbols and a different color for the house and sign.

CPSIA information can be obtained at www.ICGtesting.com
Printed in the USA
BVOW082356270313

316654BV00001B/28/P